Copyright Notice & Disclaimer

Your future performance is down to you, your attitude, your choices, your behaviours, and your consistent ability to read, relate, assimilate, and apply these PR tactics – daily.

It's time to get on point, on form & on fire with your PR.

Table of Contents

Introduction

The Covid-19 Pandemic and global economic uncertainty in the last 2 years have caused many businesses to close their doors and created 2 new breeds of entrepreneur...

h@ppeneur ® **n**. *someone who plans, documents, executes & automates their marketing online to start, grow a business and to achieve their personal goals and objectives.*

intr@preneur ® **n**. *An employee or manager within a company who plans, documents,*

executes & automates their marketing online leveraging the organisation's resources to achieve their own personal goals and the corporate objectives.

Many business owners and managers have had to revise and improve their PR Strategy to include many different approaches for raising their profile, increasing awareness,

Educate their target audience, and generating signups, appointments & sales to survive.

Imagine what...

- **...a well-placed press release could generate.**
- **...a stand at a trade show or exhibition could generate.**
- **...an article in a trade publication could generate.**
- **...an interview on radio or TV could do for your profile.**
- **...being asked as a guest blogger, panellist, or interviewee on a podcast.**
- **...being asked as a speaker at a major industry**

event could generate.

- **…an influencer's review, or video case study can do for your brand.**

Now, it is time to get on point, on form and on fire to get your message out to your audience.

 When you see this symbol throughout the book. Pause & reflect. Make notes, Answer the Question or Complete the exercise. This will assist you.

It's time to plan, document, and execute your new PR (Public Relations) Strategy. It's time to take action, to engage your audience and get seen, get heard and get paid to share your story.

And remember, if you need help, you know where I am.

Fraser J. Hay

March 2024

Possible Objectives

Welcome to "The PR Advantage," your comprehensive guide to mastering the art of Public Relations (PR) and unlocking the full potential of your brand's communication strategy.

In this chapter, we'll explore the various objectives that PR campaigns can aim to achieve, empowering you to tailor your approach and achieve maximum impact.

Imagine you're the CEO of a tech startup that's developed a revolutionary new app for managing personal finances. As you sit down with your team to plan your PR strategy, you're faced with a myriad of potential objectives. Should you focus on building brand awareness, generating leads, or fostering community engagement? Let's delve into the possibilities.

Firstly, one of the most common objectives in PR is to enhance brand visibility and awareness. Whether you're launching a new product, entering a new market, or simply seeking to increase your brand's presence, PR can help you capture the attention of your target audience. For example, a fashion brand might partner with influencers and media outlets to showcase its latest collection during Fashion Week, generating buzz and elevating its brand profile.

Next, consider the importance of reputation management as a PR objective. In today's digital age, a brand's reputation can make or break its success. PR efforts aimed at managing and enhancing reputation can involve crisis communication strategies, proactive media relations, and stakeholder engagement initiatives. Take the case of a food company facing a product recall due to safety concerns. By transparently addressing the issue, communicating corrective actions, and demonstrating a commitment to consumer safety, the brand can safeguard its reputation and regain trust.

Furthermore, PR can be instrumental in driving customer engagement and loyalty. Building meaningful relationships with your audience through authentic storytelling, interactive campaigns, and community-building initiatives can foster brand affinity and customer loyalty. For instance, a cosmetics company might launch a social media campaign inviting customers to share their makeup transformation stories, creating a sense of belonging and building a loyal community of brand advocates.

For me?

Understanding the diverse objectives that PR campaigns can aim to achieve is essential for developing strategic and impactful communication plans. Whether you're seeking to increase brand visibility, manage reputation, or foster customer engagement, PR offers a versatile toolkit to help you achieve your goals.

As you embark on your PR journey, remember to align your objectives with your overarching business goals, measure your success against predefined metrics, and continuously adapt and refine your strategies based on feedback and insights. By leveraging the power of PR to achieve your objectives, you'll gain a competitive edge and get the exposure you want.

What The experts say.

In the world of PR and communication strategy, setting clear objectives is the compass that guides every successful campaign. As renowned entrepreneur and motivational speaker, Tony Robbins once said, "*Setting goals is the first step in turning the invisible into the visible.*" This rings true for individuals and businesses alike.

By defining specific objectives in your PR efforts, you not only clarify your vision but also ignite a sense of purpose and direction. Whether it's increasing brand awareness, driving sales, or fostering community engagement, having well-defined objectives keeps you on point, on form, and on fire to achieve what you want and love to do.

Setting objectives in PR is like charting a course towards your desired destination, empowering you to navigate challenges, seize opportunities, and make your dreams a reality allowing you to hold yourself, your team or agency staff accountable.

What if this was you?

Imagine you're the owner of a small boutique hotel nestled in a bustling city. Despite offering top-notch amenities and personalised service, you're struggling to stand out in a crowded market dominated by big chain hotels. This challenge is common in the hospitality industry, where competition is fierce, and customer expectations are high.

Now, let's examine how setting specific PR objectives can help address this challenge and propel your hotel to success. Firstly, one objective could be to enhance brand visibility and awareness. By leveraging PR tactics such as media relations, influencer partnerships, and social media campaigns, you can increase your hotel's exposure and attract more guests.

Another objective could be to establish your hotel as a thought leader in the hospitality industry. By sharing valuable insights, expertise, and unique perspectives through thought leadership articles, speaking engagements, and industry collaborations, you can position your hotel as a trusted authority and attract discerning travelers seeking authentic experiences.

Furthermore, fostering community engagement could be another crucial PR objective. By actively participating in local events, supporting charitable initiatives, and building relationships with the community, you can create a strong sense of belonging and loyalty among residents and visitors alike.

What about you?

Whether it's increasing brand visibility, establishing thought leadership, or fostering community engagement, PR offers a versatile toolkit to help businesses generate exposure, backlinks, traffic, signups, sales, and revenue.

Clarity on your reasons for wanting to use PR is paramount to achieving success in your communication strategies. Before diving into PR initiatives, it's crucial to pinpoint why PR is essential for your business or personal brand.

By aligning your reasons for using PR with specific objectives, you create a roadmap for success. For instance, if your goal is to increase brand visibility, your PR strategies may focus on securing media coverage, influencer partnerships, and social media campaigns that amplify your brand's message to a wider audience. Conversely, if your objective is to drive sales, your PR efforts may prioritize product launches, promotional events, and strategic partnerships that generate buzz and drive consumer interest.

For me.

Being clear on your reasons for using PR and tying them back into specific objectives ensures that your efforts are purposeful, targeted, and aligned with your overarching goals. This clarity not only enhances the effectiveness of your PR initiatives but also maximizes the impact of your communication strategies, leading to tangible results and business success.

For example: -

What are your reasons for launching a PR Campaign? Select your reason below.

- Gets messages out   ____
- Decrease no. of complaints   ____
- Increase sales   _____
- desirable legislation passing   _____
- Increase preference   _____
- Improve employee retention   _____
- Improve customer retention   _____
- Increase attendance   _____
- Increase likelihood of   _____
- Improve customer loyalty   _____
- Improve likelihood of purchase   _____
- Attract new customers   _____
- Improve employee loyalty   _____
- Attract new prospects   _____
- Attract new donors   _____
- Increase amount of purchase   _____
- Increase donations   _____
- Increase frequency of purchase   _____
- Boosts share price   _____
- Increase profitability   _____
- Reduce turnover   ____
- Decrease time to market   ____

OTHER

- _____

Once you know what your reasons are for using PR, let's tie that back to your objectives.

After reading about the importance of defining the reasons and objectives of your PR strategy, take a moment to reflect on your own business or personal brand. Consider the stakeholders and shareholders invested in your success and their expectations for your PR efforts.

Write down three key objectives you aim to achieve with this campaign, such as increasing brand awareness, launching a new product, or building community engagement.

Next, identify the stakeholders and shareholders who would be impacted by the success of this campaign and imagine how you would communicate the objectives and expected outcomes to them.

Finally, assess how defining clear objectives enhances your ability to secure buy-in and support for your PR initiatives, reinforcing the importance of strategic planning and alignment with overarching goals.

What's Newsworthy?

In this chapter, we'll explore a fundamental question: "What makes something newsworthy?"

Imagine this scenario: You're the owner of a boutique coffee shop, brewing up artisanal blends that have garnered a loyal following in your local community. You've recently launched a new line of sustainable coffee beans sourced directly from small farms in South America. As you sip your own freshly brewed creation, you wonder, "How can I get the word out about this exciting new venture?"

Understanding what's newsworthy is crucial in PR because it determines whether your story will capture the attention of journalists, editors, and your target audience. So, let's break it down.

Firstly, newsworthiness often boils down to the concept of relevance. Is your story timely and significant to your target audience? In the case of your coffee shop, the growing consumer interest in sustainable practices and ethically sourced products makes your new line of coffee beans highly relevant. By highlighting the social and environmental impact of your initiative, you're tapping into a broader conversation that resonates with consumers.

Next, consider the element of novelty. Is your story unique or does it offer a fresh perspective on a familiar topic? For instance, let's say you're a fitness influencer launching a new workout program. Instead of simply promoting it as another fitness routine, you could emphasize the innovative approach you've taken, such as integrating virtual reality technology for immersive workouts. This unique angle sets your story apart and piques the interest of both fitness enthusiasts and tech-savvy consumers.

Furthermore, human interest plays a significant role in determining newsworthiness. Does your story evoke emotion or connect with people on a personal level? Take the example of a fashion designer who overcame adversity to launch a successful clothing line. By sharing the designer's inspiring journey and the passion behind their creations, you're creating a narrative that resonates with audiences, making it inherently newsworthy.

For me.

Understanding what's newsworthy is essential for crafting compelling PR campaigns that capture attention, spark conversation, and drive action. Whether you're promoting a product, sharing a personal story, or advocating for a cause, identifying the unique elements that make your story newsworthy is the key to PR success.

Over the years, I used PR to get featured in the online and offline media including TV, radio, and about 200 different online media outlets and platforms, and if you follow the steps I share in the book, you too could generate results like:

What is the next PR objective that you want to achieve?

Think about your audience, and your story with a view to sharing your story and publishing your content in the demand of a hungry audience – online and offline. take a reflective moment to anchor your PR efforts in purpose and precision.

Delve into your audience's needs and desires, crafting a narrative that resonates both online and offline. In envisioning your PR strategy, prioritise having a clear reason and setting specific objectives.

Consider the hungry appetite of your audience for authentic, compelling content. With this understanding, articulate three concrete objectives for your next PR campaign, ensuring they align with overarching business goals. By embracing PR to get seen, get heard and get paid doing what you love to do, you pave the path for impactful storytelling and resonant engagement with your intended audience.

So, as you embark on your PR journey, remember to ask yourself: What makes my story timely, unique, and emotionally engaging? By answering this question, you'll unlock the power of newsworthiness and harness it to your advantage in the dynamic world of PR.

What the experts say,

Understanding what is newsworthy is the cornerstone of a successful PR and communication strategy. As Seth Godin, renowned marketer, and author, once said,

"*News is what people talk about and what journalists write about. The rest is just advertising.*" This insightful quote underscores the importance of identifying stories and angles that capture the attention of both the media and your target audience.

In PR, leveraging newsworthy content ensures that your message resonates with the public and earns media coverage, amplifying your brand's visibility and credibility. By crafting stories that are timely, relevant, and impactful, you position yourself as a thought leader and generate buzz around your brand. Ultimately, embracing the principle of newsworthiness empowers you to cut through the noise, connect with your audience, and drive meaningful engagement with your PR and communication efforts.

Now you know your reasons, you need to consider what you want to tell the media. Select your reason from the possible objectives below:

- A new or improved product
- Letter to the editor
- Anniversary
- Appointments & Promotions of staff
- Introduction of a new service
- New campaign
- New merchandising
- Changing the company image
- Changing the product image
- Company growth
- New or improved facilities
- New Free item of Value / Demo
- New markets
- Awards
- Praising / condemning something
- Conducted research.
- Start or finish of a project.
- Price and sales issues
- Annual shareholder's meetings

- Financial statements

- Mergers/acquisitions, Redundancies

- Sales and earnings / Share Price

- Guest Columnist /Guest Blogger

- Capital investment.

- Public appearance/Speaking Engagement

- Open Day

- Record Achievement

- Charitable Donation

- Employee activities

- Authored a book / report.

- Commenting on Competitors

- Industry Roundup / Market Roundup

After considering the above options and choices about "what's newsworthy" for your PR strategy," take a moment to analyse recent news stories in your industry or niche. Identify three examples of news items that garnered significant attention and discuss why they were considered newsworthy.

Consider factors such as timeliness, relevance, human interest, and impact. Next, envision how you can apply these principles to your own PR efforts. Brainstorm potential story angles or events within your organization that align with these criteria and have the potential to capture media attention and engage your target audience.

Finally, reflect on the expectations of your

stakeholders and consider how effectively leveraging newsworthiness can enhance your credibility, reputation, and overall success in PR.

.

How will you measure your success?

In this chapter, we'll explore the critical question: How will you measure your PR success?

Gone are the days of vague impressions and fuzzy results. Today, businesses and individuals alike demand tangible metrics and clear indicators of PR impact. Whether you're launching a new product, managing a crisis, or building brand awareness, understanding how to measure your PR success is essential for evaluating your efforts, refining your strategies, and demonstrating value to stakeholders.

Imagine you're the marketing director of a tech startup preparing to unveil your latest innovation to the world. As excitement builds and anticipation mounts, you recognize the importance of tracking key metrics to gauge the effectiveness of your PR campaign. From media mentions and social media engagement to website traffic and lead generation, there are numerous metrics to consider when measuring PR success.

For example, you might track the number of articles featuring your product in prominent tech publications, the reach and engagement of your social media posts announcing the launch, or the conversion rate of website visitors into customers.

In the healthcare industry, a hospital launching a public health awareness campaign may measure success by the number of community members reached, the level of engagement with educational materials, and the increase in appointments for preventive screenings. Similarly, a fashion brand launching a sustainability initiative might track metrics such as media coverage, consumer sentiment, and sales of eco-friendly products.

By identifying relevant Key Performance Indicators (KPIs) and milestones upfront, you can establish benchmarks for success and track progress towards your PR objectives. This not only helps you evaluate the effectiveness of your PR efforts but also informs future strategies and investments. Additionally, measuring PR success allows you to communicate the value of PR initiatives to stakeholders, whether it's demonstrating ROI to executives or showcasing impact to clients and partners.

Let's delve into specific metrics, KPIs, and milestones to consider when measuring PR success across various industries and scenarios. From traditional media coverage to digital analytics, we'll provide practical guidance and real-world examples to empower you to effectively evaluate and optimize your PR efforts for maximum impact and results.

Think of all the KPIs (Key Performance Indicators) you will use to measure your campaign.

Possible Key Performance Indicator (KPI)

- Square Centimetre Columns
- Articles Published
- Press releases published.
- No. Sales
- No. New Customers
- No. Leads
- No. Signups/registrations
- No. Downloads via website
- No. Phone Calls
- No. Written Enquiries in
- No. Visitors/Hits/Impressions

- No. Comments / Likes
- No. Links/Trackbacks
- SEO Rankings
- No. Subscribers
- No. Followers/Friends
- No. Shares / reshares
- No. Document Downloads
- No. Channel Subscribers
- No. Ezine Subscribers
- No. Views
- No. Interviews
- No. JV Requests
- No. Speaker Requests
- No. Members to website

Media monitoring tools can play a pivotal role in assessing the reach and resonance of your PR campaigns. Platforms like Meltwater and Cision offer comprehensive media monitoring services, allowing you to track mentions of your brand or key messages across print, online, and broadcast media outlets. These tools provide valuable insights into media coverage volume, sentiment, and audience demographics, helping you gauge the effectiveness of your PR efforts and identify areas for improvement.

Social media analytics tools are another essential resource for measuring PR effectiveness in the digital age. Platforms like Hootsuite and Sprout Social offer robust analytics dashboards that allow you to track key metrics such as engagement, reach, and sentiment across various social media platforms. By monitoring trends, analyzing audience behavior, and tracking the performance of your social media content, you can gain valuable insights into the effectiveness of your PR campaigns and refine your social media strategy accordingly.

Web analytics platforms like Google Analytics provide invaluable insights into the impact of your PR efforts on website traffic and conversions. By tracking metrics such as website visits, page views, and conversion rates, you can measure the direct impact of PR initiatives on driving online engagement and conversions.

Additionally, tools like Bitly and UTM parameters allow you to track the effectiveness of specific PR campaigns or initiatives by generating custom tracking links that capture data on click-through rates and conversion metrics.

In conclusion, measuring PR effectiveness is essential for evaluating the impact of your communication strategies, refining your approach, and demonstrating the value of PR to stakeholders. By leveraging media monitoring tools, social media analytics platforms, and web analytics resources, you can track key metrics, identify areas for improvement, and optimize your PR efforts for maximum impact and success.

Here are some online resources you can explore:

Meltwater: A media monitoring platform that tracks mentions of your brand or key messages across various media outlets.

Cision: Another media monitoring service that provides comprehensive coverage and analysis of media mentions.

Hootsuite: A social media management platform that offers robust analytics dashboards for tracking social media performance.

Sprout Social: Like Hootsuite, Sprout Social provides social media analytics and management tools to help you measure the effectiveness of your PR campaigns.

Google Analytics: A web analytics platform that tracks website traffic, user behavior, and conversions, allowing you to measure the impact of your PR efforts on website performance.

Bitly: A URL shortening service that allows you to track the performance of custom tracking links, including click-through rates and conversion metrics.

A common way to measure success in the press is to measure how much "space" or coverage you have achieved, then viewing their rate card for advertising, work out how much it would cost you to buy the same space.

The same can also be done for TV and radio coverage too, simply compare how much it would cost you to buy the same amount of "minutes" airtime.

If your call to action in your press release, articles, videos, reports etc. is to direct people to a particular page on website, then install Google Analytics on your website. Google Analytics is a **FREE** enterprise-class web analytics solution that gives you rich insights into your website traffic and marketing effectiveness.

Powerful, flexible, and easy-to-use features now let you see and analyze your traffic data in an entirely new way. With Google Analytics, you're more prepared to write better-targeted ads, strengthen your marketing initiatives and create higher converting websites:

https://marketingplatform.google.com/about/

Take a moment to apply what you've just read to your own PR strategy. Start by identifying three key objectives for your upcoming PR campaign, considering factors such as brand awareness, reputation management, and audience engagement.

Next, brainstorm specific metrics and KPIs that align with each objective, keeping in mind the expectations of your stakeholders and the needs of your target audience. For example, if your objective is to increase brand awareness, consider metrics such as media mentions, social media impressions, and website traffic.

Finally, outline a plan for how you will track and evaluate these metrics throughout the campaign, ensuring that you have the tools and resources in place to measure PR effectiveness accurately. By defining clear objectives and metrics upfront, you'll not only strengthen your PR strategy but also demonstrate accountability and drive tangible results for your organisation.

Who Are Your Publics?

In this chapter, we'll delve into the importance of identifying and understanding the three key types of publics you want to reach with your PR efforts. These publics encompass distinct groups of individuals and stakeholders who play a crucial role in shaping perceptions, driving engagement, and achieving your PR objectives.

Imagine you're the communications manager for a leading consumer electronics company gearing up for the launch of its latest smartphone. Your target audiences extend beyond just potential customers—they also include media professionals, industry influencers, and internal stakeholders. Let's explore each of these publics in detail and why they're essential for PR success.

Media Professionals: This group comprises journalists, editors, bloggers, and other members of the media who have the power to amplify your message and shape public opinion. Securing positive media coverage is crucial for generating buzz, building credibility, and reaching a wider audience. For example, a tech company launching a groundbreaking innovation would target tech journalists and influencers to ensure widespread coverage and visibility within the industry.

Industry Influencers: Influencers, thought leaders, and subject matter experts within your industry or niche can be invaluable allies in your PR efforts. By leveraging their expertise, reach, and credibility, you can amplify your message, gain endorsements, and build trust with your target audience. For instance, a beauty brand launching a new skincare line might partner with beauty bloggers and social media influencers to generate buzz and drive sales among their followers.

Internal Stakeholders: Your internal stakeholders, including employees, investors, and business partners, are essential advocates and ambassadors for your brand. Keeping them informed, engaged, and aligned with your PR goals is crucial for fostering loyalty, driving employee morale, and maintaining investor confidence. For example, a pharmaceutical company announcing a breakthrough in drug development would communicate the news internally to employees, ensuring they are informed and enthusiastic about the company's achievements.

For me, identifying and reaching the three types of publics—media professionals, industry influencers, and internal stakeholders—is essential for PR success. By understanding their needs, preferences, and motivations, you can tailor your messages, tactics, and channels to effectively engage and influence each group, driving meaningful results and maximizing the impact of your PR efforts.

What the experts say

"In PR and communication strategy, understanding your publics and audiences is paramount for crafting effective messages and achieving your communication goals," says Gini Dietrich, CEO of Spin Sucks. *"Each public or audience segment has unique needs, preferences, and communication channels. By conducting thorough audience research and segmentation, you can tailor your messaging to resonate with each group, increasing the likelihood of engagement and positive outcomes."*

This insight highlights the importance of audience-centric communication in PR and emphasizes the role of audience analysis in guiding strategic decision-making. By prioritizing audience understanding and segmentation, individuals and organizations can effectively connect with their target audiences, drive meaningful engagement, and achieve success in their PR and communication efforts.

You need to identify who your target audience/public is. There are 3 types of "Publics":

Latent publics represent an audience with unacknowledged needs or challenges, unaware of their potential problem until brought to their attention. These individuals may be oblivious to a solution that could significantly enhance their lives or address an underlying issue. For instance, consider a software company offering a novel productivity tool targeting individuals struggling with time management.

Despite facing inefficiencies, many potential users may not recognize their need for such a solution until exposed to it. By identifying and tapping into latent publics, businesses can proactively address latent needs, effectively positioning their offerings as solutions before their audience even realizes they have a problem. This proactive approach can lead to early adoption, customer loyalty, and a competitive edge in the market.

Who are you wishing to target and reach?

_____

_____

_____

Aware publics denote groups that acknowledge the existence of a problem or challenge within their lives or communities. These individuals are conscious of the issue at hand and may actively seek solutions or support to address it.

For instance, in the realm of environmental sustainability, aware publics could include individuals who recognize the pressing need to reduce plastic waste and actively engage in recycling programs or advocate for eco-friendly alternatives. Similarly, within the healthcare sector, aware publics may consist of patients diagnosed with a particular illness who are actively seeking treatment options and support networks.

By understanding and engaging with aware publics, organizations can tailor their messaging and initiatives to resonate with their concerns, fostering meaningful connections and driving positive change.

Who are you wishing to target and reach?

_____

_____

_____

Active publics are groups that are actively engaged in addressing a problem or issue, taking tangible steps to enact change or find solutions. These individuals are proactive in their efforts and may participate in advocacy, activism, or community initiatives to effectuate positive outcomes.

For instance, within the realm of social justice, active publics may include grassroots organizations organizing protests or campaigns to raise awareness and advocate for policy reform. In the context of public health, active publics could consist of volunteers working to promote vaccination drives or educate communities about preventive measures against diseases.

By recognising and supporting active publics, organisations can collaborate with motivated individuals to drive meaningful change and create a lasting impact within their communities.

Who are you wishing to target and reach?

_____

_____

_____

Some useful resources.

Here are some useful resources to help you define your publics and audience:

HubSpot's Make My Persona: HubSpot offers a free tool called "Make My Persona" that guides users through the process of creating detailed buyer personas. It provides templates, prompts, and examples to help define audience demographics, goals, challenges, and preferences.

Xtensio: Xtensio is a collaborative platform that offers customizable templates for creating various business documents, including audience personas. Users can easily create detailed personas by filling in predefined sections covering demographics, psychographics, behaviors, goals, and pain points.

Canva: Canva is a versatile graphic design tool that offers pre-designed templates for creating visually appealing audience personas. Users can customize these templates with information about their target audience's demographics, interests, preferences, and motivations.

PersonaBold: PersonaBold is a user-friendly online tool specifically designed for creating audience personas. It provides customizable templates and prompts for defining audience characteristics, behaviors, goals, challenges, and preferences. Users can easily create, edit, and share personas with their teams.

UserForge: UserForge is a comprehensive user research platform that offers tools for creating detailed audience profiles and personas. It provides features for collecting and analyzing user data, conducting surveys and interviews, and visualizing audience insights to inform persona creation.

These resources offer valuable tools and templates to streamline the process of creating audience profiles and personas, allowing businesses to gain deeper insights into their target audience and tailor their marketing and communication strategies accordingly.

Try and create a profile of who your intended audience is. Think about Geographic, Demographic, Psychographic and behavioural considerations. Please be as specific as possible, this will help you.

 Take a moment to conduct an audience analysis for your own PR strategy. Start by identifying the key stakeholders and target audiences relevant to your industry or organisation. Consider their demographics, interests, needs, and communication preferences.

Then, create audience personas for each group, incorporating details such as age, gender, profession, motivations, and pain points.

Finally, imagine how you would tailor your messaging and tactics to resonate with each audience segment, addressing their specific concerns and aspirations. By taking a strategic approach to audience definition, you'll ensure that your PR efforts are targeted, relevant, and impactful, driving meaningful engagement and achieving your communication goals.

Fraserism No. 184

CRAFT YOUR STORY WITH INTENTION, FOR IT HAS THE POWER TO INSPIRE, INFLUENCE, AND IGNITE CHANGE

it stacks up.

Get on point, on form & on fire at itstacksup.com

Who Are Your Stakeholders?

Whether you're crafting a press release or orchestrating a PR campaign, each stakeholder group plays a crucial role in shaping perceptions, driving engagement, and achieving your communication goals. Let's explore the various stakeholders involved and how they can impact your PR efforts.

Staff

Your employees are the backbone of your organisation, and they can be both recipients and contributors to your PR efforts. When crafting a press release or PR campaign, consider how it may affect specific employees within your organisation.

For example, a company-wide announcement about a new product launch may excite your sales team, motivating them to promote the product to customers. Conversely, news of a restructuring or downsizing may provoke anxiety or uncertainty among staff members, necessitating transparent communication and employee support initiatives.

List your stakeholders:

_____

_____

_____

Suppliers

Your suppliers are essential partners in your business

ecosystem, and their perception of your organization can impact your reputation and relationships. When planning a press release or PR campaign, consider how it may affect specific suppliers or vendors. For instance, announcing a major partnership or collaboration may strengthen your relationships with key suppliers, leading to enhanced cooperation and support. Conversely, negative publicity or controversy surrounding your organisation may cause suppliers to reassess their association with your brand, potentially affecting supply chain dynamics and operations.

List your stakeholders:

Management Team

Your management team comprises key decision-makers and leaders within your organization, and their alignment and support are critical for PR success. When developing a press release or PR campaign, consider how it may impact your management team's reputation, credibility, and strategic objectives. For example, highlighting the achievements or thought leadership of your executives in a press release can enhance their visibility and influence within their respective industries. Conversely, mishandled communications or controversies involving your management team may damage their reputation and erode stakeholder trust.

List your stakeholders:

Investors.

Your investors are crucial stakeholders who provide financial support and strategic guidance to your organization, and their confidence in your brand can impact your market value and growth prospects. When crafting a press release or PR campaign, consider how it may affect specific investors or shareholder groups. For example, announcing strong financial results or strategic initiatives may bolster investor confidence and attract new investment. Conversely, negative publicity or scandals may trigger investor concerns and lead to stock price volatility or shareholder activism.

List your stakeholders:

_____

_____

_____

Partners

Your channel and joint venture partners are valuable allies who collaborate with your organization to deliver products or services to customers. When planning a press release or PR campaign, consider how it may impact specific partners or partner organizations. For example, announcing a new product or service offering may create opportunities for cross-promotion and co-marketing initiatives with your partners. Conversely, conflicts or disputes with partners may strain relationships and jeopardize future collaborations, requiring effective communication and conflict resolution strategies.

List your stakeholders:

_____

_____

For me, understanding your stakeholders is essential for crafting effective PR campaigns that resonate with your target audience and achieve your communication objectives.

By considering the perspectives, interests, and concerns of each stakeholder group, you can tailor your messaging, tactics, and channels to effectively engage and influence key stakeholders, driving positive outcomes and fostering long-term relationships.

Think about all those that have an "interest" in the story, or who could offer a quote or case study.

 Ensure you take notes and reflect on the above. Discuss the points with other members of your team. Have you completed the exercise above?

    0. Not Applicable.

    1. Yes. All done & documented.

    2. On the case. Working towards it, documenting it.

    3. Oops. No, not yet completed (or started).

    4. This is all too overwhelming. I Need help with iis – fast.

Conduct a Media Audit

In this chapter, we'll look at the importance of conducting a media audit—a systematic review and analysis of media outlets and channels—to identify potential media targets for your content and campaigns.

Imagine you're the PR manager for a leading fashion brand preparing to launch a new clothing line. Your goal is to generate buzz and visibility for the collection by securing media coverage across various outlets. Conducting a media audit allows you to identify relevant journalists, bloggers, influencers, and publications covering fashion and lifestyle topics. By analyzing factors such as audience demographics, content focus, editorial style, and engagement metrics, you can pinpoint the most suitable media targets to reach your desired audience effectively.

In the healthcare industry, conducting a media audit can help pharmaceutical companies identify medical journals, healthcare blogs, and online forums frequented by healthcare professionals and patients. By understanding the preferences and interests of these audiences, organizations can tailor their PR efforts to deliver relevant and valuable content that resonates with key stakeholders.

In the technology sector, media audits enable software companies to identify tech journalists, industry analysts, and technology influencers covering emerging trends and innovations. By monitoring the editorial calendars and content themes of relevant media outlets, organizations can strategically time their PR campaigns to coincide with new product launches or industry events, maximizing media coverage and visibility.

In academia, media audits help universities and research institutions identify academic journals, education blogs, and media outlets specializing in higher education topics. By leveraging these media targets, organizations can amplify their research findings, thought leadership initiatives, and academic achievements to reach a wider audience and enhance their reputation within the academic community.

For me, conducting a media audit is a vital step in shaping your PR strategy and identifying the most effective media targets for your content and campaigns. By leveraging insights from media audits, organizations can strategically engage with journalists, bloggers, influencers, and publications that align with their goals and target audience, driving visibility, credibility, and impact for their brand or organization.

Some useful resources

These online media database and media research resources provide valuable insights and data for conducting comprehensive media audits, tracking media coverage, and optimizing PR strategies to achieve communication goals:

Muck Rack offers a comprehensive media database and monitoring platform that allows users to discover journalists, track media mentions, and analyse coverage trends. PR professionals can use Muck Rack to research media contacts, pitch stories, and measure the impact of their PR efforts.

MediaMiser provides media monitoring and analysis

solutions that enable organizations to track and analyze media coverage across print, online, and social media channels. With its comprehensive database of media outlets and journalists, MediaMiser helps PR professionals identify media opportunities and assess campaign effectiveness.

Vuelio offers media database and PR software solutions designed to help PR professionals identify influencers, track media coverage, and manage media relations. With its extensive database of journalists, bloggers, and social media influencers, Vuelio provides valuable insights for media audits and PR planning.

Burrelles offers media monitoring and measurement services that help PR professionals track media coverage, analyze sentiment, and measure campaign impact. With its media database and monitoring tools, Burrelles provides comprehensive coverage across print, online, broadcast, and social media channels.

TrendKitete offers media monitoring and analytics solutions designed to help PR professionals measure and optimize their PR efforts. With its media database and AI-powered analytics platform, TrendKite provides insights into media coverage, audience engagement, and campaign effectiveness.

LexisNexis Newsdesk is a media monitoring and research platform that provides access to a vast database of news sources, including newspapers, magazines, wire services, and online news sites. PR professionals can use Newsdesk to track media coverage, monitor competitors, and analyze industry trends.

Critical Mention offers real-time media monitoring and analytics tools that enable organizations to track TV, radio, online news, and social media mentions. With its comprehensive coverage and analytics capabilities, Critical Mention helps PR professionals track media coverage, measure brand sentiment, and identify emerging trends.

. Use the space below to highlight which media outlets you will target and why. You may want to refer to the list of resources on the next page to help you.

Understanding your target audience is crucial in crafting an effective PR strategy. Once you've identified your publics, the next step is to determine which media outlets align with their preferences and interests. By targeting the right newspapers, magazines, TV, radio stations, and websites, you can maximise the reach and impact of your PR efforts.

INDUSTRY PUBLICATIONS / WEBSITES / MEDIA OUTLETS

Title/Outlet: [Name of Industry Publication]

Circulation/Audience Size: [Circulation or Audience Size]

Why Target: This publication is a leading source of industry news and insights, trusted by professionals and decision-makers in our field. By securing coverage here, we can establish credibility and reach a highly targeted audience interested in our niche offerings.

Title/Outlet: [Name of Industry Website]

Circulation/Audience Size: [Circulation or Audience Size]

Why Target: With its extensive online reach and engaged user base, this website serves as a valuable platform to share thought leadership content and promote our brand to industry stakeholders.

Title/Outlet: [Name of Trade Magazine]

Circulation/Audience Size: [Circulation or Audience Size]

Why Target: This trade magazine boasts a loyal readership among professionals in our

sector. By securing coverage here, we can position ourselves as industry experts and gain visibility among key decision-makers.

Title/Outlet: [Name of Industry Blog]

Circulation/Audience Size: [Circulation or Audience Size]

Why Target: This popular industry blog attracts a diverse audience of professionals seeking practical insights and best practices. By contributing guest posts or sponsoring content, we can engage with our target audience in a more interactive and relatable manner.

Title/Outlet: [Name of Industry Podcast]

Circulation/Audience Size: [Circulation or Audience Size]

Why Target: With its growing listenership and influential hosts, this industry podcast offers a unique opportunity to share our brand story and expertise through audio content, reaching audiences on the go.

CUSTOMER PUBLICATIONS / WEBSITES / MEDIA OUTLETS

[Repeat the same format as above, tailored to media outlets targeting your customers.]

GENERAL PUBLICATIONS / WEBSITES / MEDIA OUTLETS

[Repeat the same format as above, tailored to general media outlets that reach a broader audience.]

To assist in identifying suitable media targets, utilize online resources such as media databases, industry directories, and PR tools. Platforms like Cision, Muck Rack, and HARO (Help a Reporter Out) provide comprehensive databases of journalists, media outlets, and editorial calendars, allowing you to research and connect with relevant contacts. Additionally, industry-specific directories and forums can offer valuable insights into niche publications and digital communities frequented by your target audience. By leveraging these resources, you can streamline the process of identifying and engaging with media outlets that align with your PR objectives and audience demographics.

Take a moment to create a media audit checklist tailored to your organization's goals and target audience.

List the key media outlets, journalists, and influencers relevant to your industry and audience, and prioritise them based on their reach and engagement. Then, set aside time each month to review your media audit checklist and track your progress in securing media coverage and engaging with key stakeholders.

By regularly revisiting and updating your media audit, you'll ensure that your PR efforts remain aligned with your strategic objectives and that you're maximising your impact and reach.

Media Audit - Resources

Some additional resources that may help you:

Newspaper Society Database - www.nsdatabase.co.uk

This database offers comprehensive information on newspapers in the UK, making it an excellent starting point for understanding the media landscape and identifying potential outlets for your PR campaigns.

Online Public Relations - www.online-pr.com

Online PR provides a wealth of tools, documents, and resources for PR professionals, offering valuable insights and strategies to enhance your PR efforts and achieve your communication goals.

Radio Stations - https://www.radiocentre.org/

For those looking to expand their reach to radio, this site offers valuable demographic information and insights into the best radio stations to target for advertising, helping you effectively reach your target audience.

Media Info - https://media.info/

Media Info is a powerful database that allows you to search for TV and radio stations, newspapers, and magazines by keywords, regions, counties, and sectors, providing valuable insights for planning targeted PR campaigns.

OdwyerPR - https://www.odwyerpr.com/

OdwyerPR is a valuable resource for finding PR agencies, allowing you to connect with experienced professionals who can help you execute successful PR campaigns and achieve your communication objectives.

Digital Spy - www.digitalspy.co.uk

Digital Spy offers insights into upcoming TV shows and production trends, helping you stay informed about relevant opportunities for media coverage and publicity.

Slideshare – https://www.slideshare.net

By uploading your press releases to SlideShare, you can leverage this platform to enhance your online presence, generate backlinks, and reach a wider audience through integration with your LinkedIn profile.

Press Plugs - https://pressplugs.co.uk/

Press Plugs connects reporters with experts like you, providing opportunities to contribute insights, expertise, and commentary to media outlets seeking content contributors.

HARO - https://www.helpareporter.com/

HARO (Help a Reporter Out) connects journalists with expert sources, offering opportunities for you to contribute to media stories and gain valuable exposure for your expertise and brand.

News Now - www.newsnow.co.uk

News Now offers a platform for exploring various news topics and trends, providing inspiration and ideas for your promotional campaigns and content strategy.

Post Planner - https://www.postplanner.com/

Post Planner is a valuable tool for increasing engagement on social media platforms, offering features and strategies to optimize your content and maximize its impact on your audience.

Fraserism No. 190

HARNESS THE TRANSFORMATIVE POTENTIAL OF THE MEDIA TO ELEVATE VOICES, CHAMPION CAUSES, AND EFFECT POSITIVE CHANGE IN SOCIETY

it stacks up.

Get on point, on form & on fire at itstacksup.com

You Must Have a Story to Tell

Crafting compelling narratives isn't just an option; it's a necessity for success. Imagine yourself as a budding entrepreneur in the food industry, eager to get your artisanal jam brand noticed by the media. You've poured your heart and soul into perfecting your recipes, but now you face the challenge of standing out in a crowded market.

How do you do it? Simple. You tell a story.

Storytelling reigns supreme and holds the key to unlocking the door to media coverage and mentions. Welcome to the dynamic realm of storytelling, where the magic happens, and the media and consumers alike eagerly await captivating narratives. Picture yourself as a budding entrepreneur in the tech industry, brimming with excitement about your revolutionary new app. You've poured your heart and soul into developing this game-changing solution, but now comes the crucial step: crafting a compelling story that will capture the attention of the media and resonate with your target audience.

So, what are the essential elements that the media and consumers crave in a good story?

First, authenticity reigns supreme. Take the success story of Airbnb, for example. Founded by Brian Chesky and Joe Gebbia, Airbnb didn't just offer accommodations; it offered unique, authentic experiences that resonated with travelers worldwide. By sharing the stories of their hosts and the communities they served, Airbnb tapped into the power of authenticity and created a global movement that transcended traditional hospitality.

Next up, relevance is key. Consider the rise of Dollar Shave Club, a subscription-based razor company that disrupted the shaving industry with its quirky marketing campaigns and relatable brand persona. By addressing a common pain point—overpriced razors—and offering a convenient, affordable solution, Dollar Shave Club captured the attention of both consumers and the media, leading to its acquisition by Unilever for $1 billion.

But what about emotional appeal? Look no further than the viral sensation of the ALS Ice Bucket Challenge. What started as a grassroots campaign to raise awareness and funds for amyotrophic lateral sclerosis (ALS) quickly became a global phenomenon, thanks to its emotional resonance and widespread social media sharing. By tapping into the power of human connection and empathy, the ALS Association raised over $115 million and sparked conversations around the world.

Additionally, storytelling in the digital age requires multimedia elements to truly captivate audiences.

Take the example of Red Bull's Stratos project, which saw Austrian skydiver Felix Baumgartner jump from the edge of space. By live streaming the event on YouTube and incorporating stunning visuals and real-time updates, Red Bull engaged millions of viewers and generated massive media coverage, solidifying its reputation as a leader in extreme sports marketing.

Finally, a successful story must have a clear call to action. Look at the impact of Nike's "Just Do It" campaign, which inspired athletes of all levels to push their limits and strive for greatness. By empowering consumers to take action and pursue their dreams, Nike not only built a loyal customer base but also cemented its position as a cultural icon.

For me? The important elements that the media and consumers want in a good story are authenticity, relevance, emotional appeal, multimedia engagement, and a compelling call to action. By incorporating these elements into your storytelling efforts, you can create stories that resonate with your audience, attract media attention, and drive meaningful impact for your brand.

I've shared my story in my books, blogs, interviews and TEDx talk, but what about you? What's your story?

It's time to share it with the world.

But storytelling isn't limited to traditional media outlets. In today's digital age, social media platforms offer a powerful platform for sharing your brand's story with the world. Imagine you're a sustainable skincare brand looking to connect with environmentally conscious consumers.

Through visually stunning imagery and captivating captions, you share the story of your brand's commitment to sustainability, from ethically sourced ingredients to eco-friendly packaging.

By tapping into the emotions of eco-conscious consumers and aligning with their values, you not only attract a loyal following on social media but also catch the attention of influencers and media outlets looking for brands with a compelling narrative.

So why is storytelling so essential in PR? Simply put, stories have the power to captivate, inspire, and resonate with audiences on a profound level. In a world inundated with information and advertising, stories cut through the clutter and create genuine connections with consumers and journalists alike.

By weaving narratives that evoke emotion, spark conversation, and convey the essence of your brand, you can elevate your PR efforts, attract media coverage, and leave an impression in the minds of your audience. So, remember, in the realm of PR, you must have a story to tell. It's not just a luxury; it's a necessity for success.

Key Elements of a Good Story for The Media

Newsworthiness: The story must be timely, relevant, and have a unique angle that captures the attention of the audience. It should address current events, trends, or issues that are of interest to the public.

Human interest: Stories that evoke emotions such as empathy, inspiration, or curiosity are more likely to resonate with audiences. Including personal anecdotes, testimonials, or human experiences can make the story relatable and engaging.

Conflict or controversy: Media outlets are often drawn to stories that involve conflict, controversy, or drama. However, it's essential to ensure that the conflict is handled sensitively and ethically, without causing harm or sensationalizing the issue.

Clear storytelling: A well-structured narrative with a clear beginning, middle, and end helps readers follow the story and stay engaged. Avoiding jargon or technical language and using simple, concise language enhances readability and accessibility.

Visual elements: Incorporating visuals such as photographs, videos, infographics, or illustrations can enhance the storytelling experience and make the story more compelling. Visuals help to break up the text, add context, and provide additional information to the audience.

Credible sources: Including quotes, statistics, or expert opinions from credible sources adds credibility and authority to the story. Media outlets are more likely to publish stories that are well-researched and supported by reliable sources.

Local relevance: Stories that have a local angle or impact are often more appealing to regional or community-based media outlets. Highlighting how the story relates to the local community or addressing local concerns can increase its newsworthiness.

Call to action: Ending the story with a clear call to action encourages readers to engage further with the content or take specific steps, such as visiting a website, signing a petition, or attending an event. A compelling call to action motivates readers to become active participants in the story.

Overall, a good story for the media to publish and share is one that is newsworthy, emotionally engaging, well-structured, supported by credible sources, visually appealing, locally relevant, and includes a clear call to action. By incorporating these key elements, you can increase the chances of your story being picked up and shared by media outlets.

What the experts say

Crafting a good story is essential for getting seen, heard, and becoming famous. As renowned author and marketing expert Seth Godin once said, "*People do not buy goods and services. They buy relations, stories, and magic.*"

This insightful statement underscores the power of storytelling in capturing the attention of audiences and building lasting connections. A good story resonates with emotions, sparks curiosity, and leaves an impression on the minds of consumers and media alike. By mastering the art of storytelling, individuals and brands can differentiate themselves from the competition, attract media coverage, and achieve fame and recognition.

In today's hectic and stressful climate, where attention is scarce and competition is fierce, a compelling story is the key to standing out and making a meaningful impact.

One final thing

To get your story   published or promoted by the media, you need to ensure that your story satisfies two key points: Now it's time to pick Key Media Outlets and find out their editorial guidelines.

1. **It's of interest to the media that you are targeting. It must be relevant to them & their audience.**

2. **You are actively promoting you, your services or business in a positive light.**

You do, however, must ensure that you fuse these two points together when writing your press release.

Use the following space to identify what **Editors** want: (Read different titles to get a flavour for content)

TITLE / OUTLET	Circulation / Audience Size	Editorial Guidelines / (Topics of interest)

TIP: Ensure your story is relevant to the media outlet you are targeting.

Many titles have editorial submission guidelines to follow, published on their website.

Ensure you take notes and reflect on the above. Discuss the points with other members of your team. Have you completed the exercise above?

0. Not Applicable.

1. Yes. All done & documented.

2. On the case. Working towards it, documenting it.

3. Oops. No, not yet completed (or started).

4. This is all too overwhelming. I Need help with this – fast.

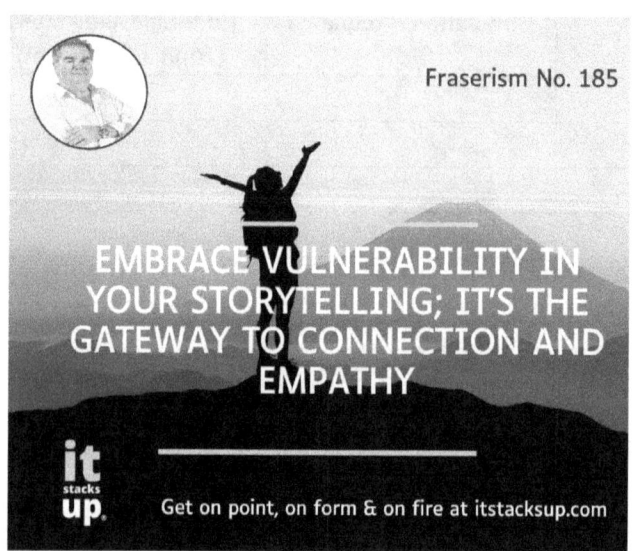

Fraserism No. 185

EMBRACE VULNERABILITY IN YOUR STORYTELLING; IT'S THE GATEWAY TO CONNECTION AND EMPATHY

it stacks **up**.

Get on point, on form & on fire at itstacksup.com

Prospects

Imagine you're browsing through your social media feed, and amidst the flood of content, one story catches your eye. It's not just any story; it's a captivating narrative that speaks directly to your interests, challenges, and aspirations. As a professional business coach, understanding why prospective customers would be interested in watching, reading, or listening to your story is paramount to your success.

Firstly, relevance is key. Consider the success of Peloton, a fitness company that has revolutionized the home workout experience. By sharing stories of real customers achieving their fitness goals with Peloton, the company not only showcases its product but also connects with potential customers on a personal level. These stories resonate because they address the universal desire for health and wellness, stirring emotions and inspiring action.

Secondly, authenticity breeds trust. Take the case of Airbnb, which disrupted the travel industry by offering unique, authentic experiences. By sharing stories of hosts and guests, Airbnb humanises its brand and builds trust with potential customers. These stories provide social proof of the value and reliability of Airbnb's platform, making it more appealing to prospective travelers.

Moreover, storytelling is a powerful tool for differentiation. Think about the success of Apple, a company renowned for its innovative products and iconic marketing campaigns. By crafting compelling stories around its products, such as the emotional "Shot on iPhone" ad campaign, Apple sets itself apart from competitors and creates a loyal following of customers who resonate with its brand values.

Additionally, addressing pain points and offering solutions can pique interest.

For example, consider the success of Slack, a communication platform that has transformed the way teams collaborate. By sharing stories of businesses streamlining their workflows and improving productivity with Slack, the company appeals to potential customers seeking more efficient ways to work.

For me, prospective customers are interested in watching, reading, or listening to your story when it resonates with their needs, stirs their emotions, and offers a solution to their challenges. By leveraging the power of storytelling to create relevant, authentic, and differentiated content, you can capture the attention and loyalty of your target audience, driving success for your business.

Why would prospective customers be interested in reading your story, article or press release?

Don't make the classic mistake about writing about product features. A good way to overcome this, and to ensure that your story, article or press release is relevant to highlight problems, issues, or challenges that the reader, listener, or viewer may be suffering from, and the benefits that your product or service offers.

Make a list of prospective problems, issues and challenges that prospective customer suffer from

_____

_____

_____

TIP: Can you quantify the impact of these problems? Journalists like facts and stats.

Referring to an actual/existing case study can be extremely useful.

Make a list of the benefits of your product, service, or solution.

_____

_____

_____

_____

TIP: If you can quantify the results generated by your product/service, the better.

Referring to an actual/existing case study can be very useful.

Ensure you take notes and reflect on the above. Discuss the points with other members of your team. Have you completed the exercise above?

0. Not Applicable.

1. Yes. All done & documented.

2. On the case. Working towards it, documenting it.

3. Oops. No, not yet completed (or started).

4. This is all too overwhelming. I Need help with this – fast.

Problems, Issues, Challenges & Reasons

When planning your PR strategy, it's crucial to understand why prospective customers would be interested in engaging with your content. Rather than focusing solely on product features, it's essential to highlight the problems, issues, or challenges that your target audience may be facing—and how your product, service, or solution provides a solution.

Let's take the example of Patagonia, a renowned outdoor clothing company. Instead of simply promoting the technical specifications of their products, Patagonia focuses on the environmental challenges faced by outdoor enthusiasts. Through compelling storytelling and impactful campaigns like "Worn Wear," which encourages customers to repair and reuse their clothing, Patagonia addresses the growing concerns about sustainability and climate change. By aligning their brand with environmental activism and offering sustainable solutions, Patagonia resonates with customers who value ethical and eco-friendly practices.

Similarly, consider the success of Slack, a communication platform for teams. Instead of merely touting its messaging features, Slack emphasizes the common challenges faced by modern workplaces, such as communication silos and information overload. Through case studies and testimonials highlighting how Slack streamlines communication and enhances productivity, the company addresses the pain points of its target audience and positions itself as a valuable solution.

By focusing on the problems, issues, and challenges that your audience encounters, you can create content that resonates on a deeper level and sparks emotional engagement. Whether it's addressing workflow inefficiencies, financial concerns, or personal struggles, showcasing how your product or service offers tangible benefits and solutions can compel prospective customers to respond to your content.

In a crowded marketplace, filled with "noise" and everyone hungry for headlines, soundbites, and attention, understanding and addressing the needs of your audience is essential for building trust, generating interest, and driving action. So, when crafting your PR strategy, remember to put the spotlight on the problems you solve and the value you provide.

Don't make the classic mistake about writing about product features. A good way to overcome this, and to ensure that your story, article or press release is relevant to highlight problems, issues, or challenges that the reader, listener, or viewer may be suffering from, and the benefits that your product or service offers.

The reader will buy after they become confident that your product or service can address or eliminate their pain. You must first demonstrate that you know what their pain is (or could be.) Your mission is to uncover as many "Motivators" as possible. One of the best ways is to ask questions, which remind the reader of their pain and how things could be with your solution. The purpose of this exercise is NOT to directly sell to them, but to ensure your focussing in on their reasons, and motivations to want to read about you and your solutions.

• **What is their Pain at Present?**	... fix this.
	...prevent this from happening.
• **Pain in the Future**	
	...prevent it from repeating itself.
• **Pain in the Past**	
• **Pleasure in the Present**	...make this happen now.
• **Pleasure in the Future**	...make it happen in the future.
• **Pleasure in the Past**	
• **Curiosity**	...remind them what others have done.
	...tease them, encourage them to want to know more

Next you can further demonstrate you understand your public's pain, for you know what symptoms or signs to look for.

So, think of specific symptoms or indicators that can remind a reader that they are "suffering" <u>now</u> and that they need to action and respond to your story, article, or press release to fix the problem.

WHAT'S DECLINING? (Sales/revenue/Profit etc.)	**WHAT'S INCREASING?** (Stress levels, costs, borrowings etc)
•	
•	
•	
•	
•	
•	

Can you make a list of specific pains, problems, needs or frustrations that your target market may have and thus, have good reasons to want to do business with you? Perhaps you have a mathematical formula that they can use or apply to calculate the true cost or impact of their pain or problem.

i.e., if a problem costs £5000, and if they don't fix it, and it occurs 3 times in 2 years, then it will cost them £15,000, but this could be avoided if....

TIP: Can you quantify the impact of these problems? Journalists like facts and stats. Referring to an actual/existing case study can be extremely useful.

Now write down the **single biggest** frustration, problem, pain or need that your public(s) have, that you know your solution can fix. (**This should be what your press release will focus on**).

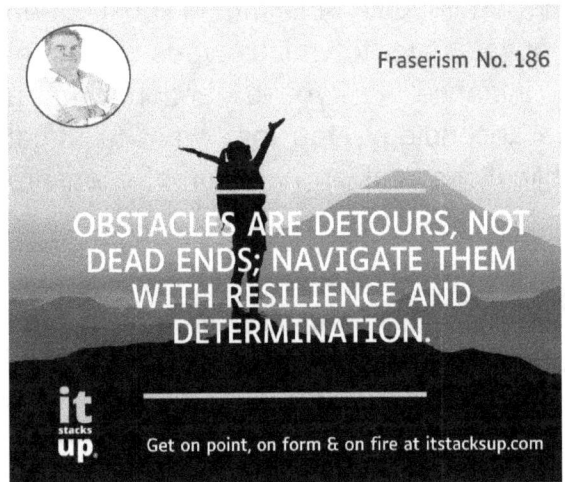

Fraserism No. 186

OBSTACLES ARE DETOURS, NOT DEAD ENDS; NAVIGATE THEM WITH RESILIENCE AND DETERMINATION.

it stacks up.

Get on point, on form & on fire at itstacksup.com

Media Outlets

Selecting the right media outlet for your PR campaign is a crucial aspect of ensuring its success and maximizing its impact. The choice of media can significantly influence the reach, effectiveness, and overall outcome of your efforts. It's essential to consider several key factors when making this decision, including your target audience, campaign objectives, and the nature of your story or message.

As previously discussed, understanding your target audience is paramount. By identifying their demographics, interests, and preferences, you can tailor your PR strategy to resonate with them effectively. For example, if your target audience consists of environmentally conscious consumers, you may want to prioritize media outlets that cover sustainability and eco-friendly initiatives.

Additionally, consider the nature of your story or message and the type of media that best complements it. Are you launching a new product, sharing an industry insight, or hosting an event? Different media outlets cater to various types of content and audiences. For instance, if you're announcing a breakthrough in medical technology, you may want to target healthcare-focused publications and online forums to ensure your message reaches relevant professionals and stakeholders.

It's also crucial to be aware of the credibility, reputation, and audience reach of potential media outlets. While securing coverage in a high-profile publication can be enticing, it's essential to ensure alignment with your brand values and campaign objectives. Conduct thorough research on each outlet's editorial focus, audience demographics, and past coverage to determine if it's a suitable fit for your message.

Additionally, consider factors such as website traffic, social media engagement, and reader engagement to gauge the potential impact of your story.

Real-life examples illustrate the importance of selecting the right media outlet. For instance, when Airbnb launched its "Live There" campaign, which encouraged travelers to experience cities like locals, they partnered with influential travel bloggers and lifestyle magazines such as Conde Nast Traveler and Travel + Leisure. By targeting media outlets that resonated with their target audience of adventurous travelers, Airbnb was able to generate widespread coverage and positive publicity for its campaign.

To assist you in selecting the right media outlet for your PR campaign, numerous online resources and tools are available. For example, tools like Agility PR Solutions provide comprehensive databases of journalists, editors, and media outlets, allowing you to research and connect with relevant contacts in your industry. Similarly, platforms like Meltwater offer media monitoring and analysis services, enabling you to track the impact of your PR efforts and measure the effectiveness of your media outreach.

For me, selecting the right media outlet for your PR campaign requires careful consideration of your target audience, campaign objectives, and the nature of your story. By understanding your audience demographics, aligning with appropriate media channels, and evaluating credibility and reach, you can maximise the effectiveness of your PR efforts and achieve your communication goals. With the help of online resources and tools, you can navigate the media landscape with confidence and successfully connect with your desired audience.

Consider tools such as:

PressRush is a media database and outreach platform that provides access to journalist contacts, editorial calendars, and media insights. It offers personalized media lists and pitching tools to help you connect with relevant journalists and influencers for your PR campaign. PressRush also offers media monitoring features to track coverage and measure the impact of your outreach efforts, making it a valuable resource for PR professionals seeking to streamline their media relations.

Prowly is a PR software platform that offers media database and outreach tools, as well as press release distribution and analytics features. It provides access to journalist contacts, media lists, and pitching templates to help you craft effective pitches and connect with the right media contacts for your campaign. Prowly also offers real-time analytics and reporting dashboards to track the performance of your PR activities and measure their impact on brand visibility and engagement.

JustReachOut is a media database and PR outreach platform that helps startups and small businesses connect with journalists and bloggers. It offers access to journalist contacts, media opportunities, and pitching templates tailored to your industry and niche. JustReachOut also provides personalized pitching advice and feedback to help you craft compelling pitches and secure media coverage for your brand or campaign. With its intuitive interface and actionable insights, JustReachOut is an ideal resource for DIY PR professionals looking to build relationships with the media and generate press coverage.

Hey Press, is a media database and outreach platform that helps startups and entrepreneurs find journalists and bloggers covering their industry or niche. It offers access to journalist contacts, media opportunities, and pitching tips to help you craft effective pitches and secure media coverage for your brand or product. Hey, Press also provides real-time alerts and notifications for relevant media opportunities, making it easy to stay updated on the latest press opportunities and trends in your industry. With its user-friendly interface and comprehensive database, Hey Press is an invaluable resource for startups and small businesses looking to generate press coverage and build brand awareness.

Publicize is a PR software platform that offers media database, outreach, and analytics tools tailored to the needs of startups and small businesses. It provides access to journalist contacts, media lists, and pitching templates designed to help you connect with relevant journalists and bloggers in your industry. Publicize also offers press release distribution services and media monitoring features to track coverage and measure the impact of your PR efforts. With its user-friendly interface and customizable features, publicize is an ideal solution for startups and small businesses looking to increase their visibility and generate press coverage.

Having Selected the Media Outlets you wish to contact, read their editorial guidelines to ensure what you are sending is relevant to them and their viewers, readers/listeners, or visitors.

If you don't know the editor/Journalist, you could simply mark it for the attention of the news desk but sending to personalised recipients will generate a much higher response/chance of your release getting published/printed/promoted/circulated.

TITLE / OUTLET	Editor / Journalist	Phone / Email / Website

 Take a moment to take notes and reflect on the above. Discuss the points with other members of your team. Have you completed the exercise above?

0. Not Applicable.

1. Yes. All done & documented.

2. On the case. Working towards it, documenting it.

3. Oops. No, not yet completed (or started).

4. This is all too overwhelming. I Need help with this – fast.

Lead Times

When writing a press release or submitting an article for publication, you need to consider lead times for certain media outlets, and publications. The following will help you as a guide Understanding the lead times of various media outlets and utilizing editorial calendars are vital components for successful PR campaigns. Let's delve into the significance of lead times, explore online resources for accessing editorial calendars, and learn how to create and manage PR calendars for optimal outreach.

Understanding Media Lead Times

Daily Newspapers operate on tight schedules, often requiring press releases to be submitted at least a day in advance of publication. For instance, if you're targeting The Washington Post or The Guardian, reaching out to editors a day prior ensures your story has a chance of making it into the next morning's edition.

Online Publications offer more flexibility in terms of lead times. Articles and press releases can be submitted at any time, allowing for immediate publishing, or scheduling for optimal visibility. Websites like PR Newswire and Business Wire provide platforms for distributing press releases to a wide range of online news outlets, offering instant exposure to target audiences.

Radio stations have varying lead time requirements, with some accepting pitches minutes before airtime and others needing more advance notice. For example, if you're pitching a story to NPR's Morning Edition, contacting producers at least a few days in advance ensures they have sufficient time to review and potentially feature your story.

Television networks typically have longer lead times compared to radio, often requiring pitches to be submitted hours or even days before scheduled airtime. Whether it's a local news segment or a national talk show appearance, coordinating with producers in advance increases the likelihood of securing TV coverage.

Magazines operate on monthly production cycles, necessitating lead times of several weeks to months in advance. Publications like Vogue or Forbes often plan editorial content well ahead of time, so pitching timely stories that align with their editorial calendars enhances the chances of coverage.

Accessing Editorial Calendars

Understanding the importance of researching and referring to editorial calendars is crucial for maximizing impact, engagement, and coverage in public relations (PR) campaigns. Editorial calendars provide valuable insights into upcoming themes and topics that media outlets plan to cover, allowing PR professionals to tailor their pitches and content accordingly.

For instance, if a tech publication is dedicating an issue to cybersecurity, aligning PR efforts with this theme increases the likelihood of securing coverage for relevant stories or expert commentary.

Online resources previously mentioned such as Help a Reporter Out (HARO), Cision, and Muck Rack offer access to editorial calendars of major publications and broadcast outlets. These platforms enable PR practitioners to stay informed about editorial opportunities, identify relevant story angles, and strategically plan their outreach efforts. By leveraging editorial calendars effectively, PR professionals can enhance their chances of success, garnering increased visibility, engagement, and credibility for their brands or clients in the media landscape.

Help a Reporter Out (HARO) is a platform connecting journalists with sources for stories. While primarily known for its query-based system, HARO also provides access to editorial calendars of various media outlets. By subscribing to HARO's premium service, PR professionals gain insights into upcoming editorial themes and topics, enabling them to tailor their pitches accordingly.

Cision is a comprehensive media database that offers access to editorial calendars of major publications and broadcast outlets. PR practitioners can leverage Cision's platform to track editorial opportunities, monitor industry trends, and plan PR campaigns effectively.

Muck Rack is a media database and PR software that provides access to editorial calendars, journalist profiles, and media monitoring tools. With Muck Rack's calendar feature, PR professionals can stay updated on upcoming editorial themes and deadlines, facilitating targeted outreach to relevant media outlets.

ContentCal is a social media and content planning tool that offers calendar-based scheduling for PR campaigns. PR teams can use ContentCal to plan and schedule press releases, blog posts, and social media content, ensuring consistent messaging and optimal timing across channels.

ResponseSource is a platform connecting journalists with expert sources and story ideas. In addition to its query service, ResponseSource offers access to editorial calendars of leading media outlets, allowing PR professionals to align their pitches with upcoming editorial themes and opportunities.

For me, mastering media lead times and leveraging editorial calendars are essential strategies for successful PR campaigns. By understanding the lead times of different media outlets and utilizing online resources to access editorial calendars, PR professionals can enhance their outreach efforts, secure media coverage, and achieve their communication objectives.

Shorten Your URLs

Shortening URLs with tracking tools is a crucial practice in PR for several reasons. Firstly, it enhances the aesthetics of links, making them more appealing and shareable across digital platforms such as social media, press releases, and email campaigns.

Additionally, URL shortening tools provide valuable analytics that enable PR professionals to track the performance of their links in real-time. By monitoring metrics like click-through rates, geographic location of users, and referral sources, PR practitioners can gain insights into audience behavior and engagement.

Examples of popular URL shortening and tracking tools include Bitly, TinyURL, and Rebrandly. These tools empower PR teams to optimize their campaigns, measure the effectiveness of their strategies, and make data-driven decisions to enhance their overall outreach and communication efforts.

This streamlined approach enhances campaign performance, facilitates data-driven decision-making, and contributes to achieving PR objectives more efficiently.

> **You can use** https://bit.ly, **https://tinyurl.com/,**
> **https://snipurl.com/**

EVERY JOURNEY STARTS WITH A SINGLE STEP, BUT IT'S THE CONSISTENT MONITORING OF THOSE STEPS THAT LEADS TO MEANINGFUL PROGRESS

Get on point, on form & on fire at itstacksup.com

What to Include in a Media Kit?

Some journalists' email inboxes get thousands of emails a day, and a powerful high responsive tactic is to send your Media Kit registered mail. Many people have forgotten just how impactful this can be. Furthermore, everyone loves getting a surprise letter in the post, especially if it is sent registered mail and it is not shocking news. Think about it.

Presentation folder

This should be a simple A4 cardboard folder. Can also be used for workshop or seminar notes and serve a whole multitude of other purposes too. Check out www.vistaprint.com for getting them printed.

Cover Letter

We strongly suggest that you either paper clip your covering letter to the outside of your presentation folder or ensure it is the first item seen when you open the folder. Your covering letter should give a good introduction.

to you and your business, also indicate your willingness and wishes to co-operate with the press.

An Executive Summary

This document is usually a 1 – 3-page summary of your business achievements and organisational profile. If you are comfortable in enclosing your annual report or P&L and balance sheet, then do so.

Fact sheet

Journalists love facts and figures, so if you have some nice summary stats, then include them.

Photos and slides

Snaps of you, your staff or products can be an especially useful addition. Either include the actual snaps or enclose a URL where the journalist can download them from your website.

Press Clippings

Contrary to widespread belief, journalists like to read other coverage that you may have had, it helps to authenticate who you are, and helps to position you as an expert.

Brochures

If you have a corporate brochure, then include it. It helps to explain who you are and what you offer.

Survey results.

If you have results of a recent survey, then include them.

Contact sheet.

Include a sheet with relevant contact information of relevant people from your organisation.

Business Card

Many presentation folders have cuts in the folder so they can store your card in a prominent place.

Your Media Site / Library

Many websites produce their own resource page for people to download the above documents as PDFs, watch videos and complete signup forms. Think how you can add this to your PR strategy.

Take a moment to develop a media kit or keynote speaker kit tailored to your goals and target audience. Start by compiling key information about your brand, such as press releases, bios, high-resolution images, and notable achievements.

Consider including testimonials, case studies, and sample interview questions to showcase your expertise and credibility. Utilize online resources like Canva or Adobe Spark to design visually appealing materials that align with your brand identity.

By creating a comprehensive media kit or keynote speaker kit, you'll be well-prepared to engage with journalists, event organizers, and potential collaborators, effectively amplifying your message and maximizing opportunities for exposure.

Authoring Articles (& Blogs) For Syndication

Authoring articles and blogs for syndication offers a powerful platform to establish yourself as an industry authority. Crafting content tailored to resonate with your target audience is paramount for engaging readers. The headline serves as a crucial gateway, offering a glimpse into the article's content while enticing readers with compelling reasons to delve deeper.

By harnessing the potential of article writing, you can enhance brand visibility, attract new audiences, and foster meaningful connections within your industry. With strategic content creation, you can unlock opportunities for thought leadership and drive tangible results for your business or personal brand.

Obviously, the content of your article should be geared towards your public and target audience.

The title/headline of your article is particularly important and not only often explains the content of the article or who it is targeted at, but also can give compelling reasons to want to read it.

Here are eight examples of several types of article headlines/titles. **(Can also be used for press releases too.)**

1. The News Headline: Ensure You Announce Why your article is newsworthy. Think how you can pull in the reader and grab their attention. Good words to use are: *New, Revolutionary, Just Released, Announcing, Introducing* etc.

- *"Announcing…. The ultimate new insect repellent for Midges"*

- *"Revolutionary new shark bait diet that's taking the USA by storm."*

- *"Just Released: Astounding facts about Social Networking that will shock You."*

TEMPLATE:

Discover Proven Method to

_____

2. The Guarantee Headline: These tend to state a desirable benefit and guarantee results or other benefits. If you can, then offer a guarantee to mitigate or eliminate risk and to instill confidence in your readers.

- *"Generate traffic to your website in less than 24 hours or your money back."*

- *"Get more miles to the gallon, or it's free with our 100% unconditional guarantee."*

TEMPLATE:

We promise to _____ or your money back.

3. The How to Headline: This is brilliant for revealing insider information. Everyone wants to know how to do something better, cheaper, quicker. If you ever get stuck, try adding 'how to' in front of your headline as these types of headlines promise your prospect a source of information, advice, and solutions to their problems.

- *"How to Make Money on Ecademy.com"*

- *"How to generate 200 suspects and 30 hot prospects in 59 minutes or less."*

- *"How to maintain an orgasm for 23 minutes and 4 seconds."'*

TEMPLATE:

How to (get) _____ in _____
(timeframe)

3. **The Benefit Headline:** Benefits sell . . . features DO NOT! Think about what your readers will get because of having used your product, service, or solution. Tell them what they can expect to empower them to take action.

- "Earn £100,000 a year as a Marketing Coach."

- *"Lose Weight, Look Good, and feel better in less than 7 days."*

TEMPLATE:

Master _____ in less than

_____

The cure for

_____

The Solution to

_____

4. **The Question Headline:** Be careful when using this one. Ensure you have a real understanding of your market. A good resource to use is www.answerthepublic.com. You can research and find out what people are asking online, then state the answer or solution in your body copy.

- *"Do you make these mistakes in English?"*

- *"Do you make these mistakes when Networking."*

- *"Do you make these 7 mistakes when booking appointments by phone."'*

TEMPLATE:

Want more _____ Need More _____?

6. The Reason Why Headline: gives prospect specific reasons why they should read your ad, sales letter, or website. These are highly effective because they contain facts and specific numbers.

- *"75 Ways to use Twitter in Business."*

- *"99 Ways to drive traffic to your website."*

- *"101 Ways to peel a grape."'*

TEMPLATE:

Little Known Ways to _____

X Ways to _____

7. The Testimonial Headline: Simply use a customer testimonial in the headline. This can be immensely powerful. The secret here is to state a specific result in each time frame.

- *"How I turned £150 in £13,000 in 3 easy steps"*

- *"£7000 in 7 Days."*

- *"15 Prospects, 7 Sales, and £4000 in less than 24hrs."'*

My Linkedin Results were poor, until I discovered...

547 reactions · 189 comments

276,930 article views   338 reshares

Yes, it's true, I wrote an article on LinkedIn that's now had over 250,000 views.

It's HERE - https://www.linkedin.com/pulse/20141119130734-3359805-my-linkedin-results-were-poor-until-i-discovered/

Useful resources

Here are some online resources you can leverage for sharing your own articles, blogs, and posts, remembering to stay focused on your story and your audience.

Medium is a popular platform for publishing articles and blogs across various topics. It offers a vast audience and opportunities for engagement through likes, comments, and shares.

LinkedIn's publishing platform, Pulse, allows users to share articles and blogs directly with their professional network. It's an excellent way to reach a targeted audience within your industry.

WordPress is a versatile platform for creating and publishing blogs. With its extensive range of themes and plugins, you can customize your blog to suit your branding and content needs.

Substack is a newsletter platform that allows writers to monetize their content through subscriptions. It's a great option for authors looking to build a dedicated audience for their articles and blogs.

X (Twitter) is a valuable tool for sharing bite-sized snippets of your articles and blogs. By sharing links and engaging with relevant hashtags and conversations, you can expand your reach and attract new readers.

Reddit offers various niche communities (subreddits) where users can share and discuss articles and blogs on specific topics. It's a great way to connect with like-minded individuals and receive feedback on your content.

Quora is a question-and-answer platform where users can share their expertise by answering questions on various topics. By including links to your articles and blogs in your responses, you can drive traffic to your content and establish yourself as a knowledgeable authority.

These resources provide practical avenues for sharing your articles and blogs with a broader audience, increasing visibility, and fostering engagement with your content.

What the experts say

Creative writing, especially in the form of articles, is a potent tool for businesses to engage with their audience and establish thought leadership. As Michael Brenner, CEO of Marketing Insider Group, rightly puts it, "Content is the emotional and informational bridge between commerce and consumer." Through well-crafted articles, businesses can share valuable insights, address customer pain points, and build trust with their audience.

These pieces serve not only to inform but also to inspire and entertain, making them essential for nurturing strong customer relationships. In today's digital age, where content is king, businesses that prioritize quality writing can effectively differentiate themselves from the competition and drive meaningful engagement. Therefore, investing in creative writing for articles is not just important—it's essential for long-term success in building brand authority and driving business growth.

Take the time to brainstorm articles and blog ideas that align with your brand's messaging and objectives. Consider topics that showcase your expertise, address common industry challenges, or offer valuable insights to your target audience.

Utilise keyword research tools like SEMrush or Google Keyword Planner to identify relevant topics and optimise your content for search engines. Once you've authored your articles, explore platforms like Medium, LinkedIn Publishing, or industry-specific blogs for syndication opportunities.

By consistently producing high-quality content and strategically syndicating it across relevant channels, you'll establish yourself as a thought leader in your industry, expand your reach, and drive traffic to your website or landing pages.

Fraserism No. 188

EMBRACE THE BLANK PAGE AS A CANVAS FOR YOUR IMAGINATION TO RUN WILD. LET YOUR CREATIVITY FLOW FREELY AND UNAPOLOGETICALLY.

it stacks up.

Get on point, on form & on fire at itstacksup.com

Speaking Engagements

Whether you're a seasoned professional or a budding entrepreneur, the platform provided by speaking engagements offers unparalleled opportunities to connect with audiences, share valuable insights, and leave an impression.

Industries across the spectrum, from technology and finance to healthcare and education, recognize the value of expert speakers who can captivate audiences and deliver impactful messages. For example, renowned speakers like Simon Sinek in leadership, Brené Brown in personal development, and Gary Vaynerchuk in marketing have carved out lucrative careers by sharing their expertise through speaking engagements.

I've also now presented on 4 continents around the globe on many different entrepreneurial topics including resilience, the entrepreneurial journey, sales, marketing, martech and ai, and of course my TEDX which was called "*From human being to human becoming*".

If you've not seen my TEDx talk yet, it's available at https://www.youtube.com/watch?v=IttJ_XNMTwU

When it comes to setting speaking fees, several factors come into play, including your level of expertise, the size and prestige of the event, and the potential impact of your message. Fees can vary widely, ranging from a few hundred dollars for local workshops or panel discussions to tens of thousands for keynote addresses at large conferences or corporate events. Additionally, speakers may charge extra for travel expenses, customized presentations, or post-event consulting services.

To determine your speaking fees, consider your unique value proposition, the demand for your expertise, and the financial expectations of your target audience.

Online resources like SpeakerHub, SpeakerMatch, and National Speakers Association (NSA) provide valuable insights and tools for pricing your speaking services competitively.

In addition to setting fees, speakers must strategically choose speaking engagements that align with their brand, target audience, and business objectives. Platforms like TEDx, industry conferences, corporate events, and educational institutions offer diverse opportunities to showcase expertise and reach new audiences. By selecting speaking opportunities that resonate with your expertise and values, you can maximize your impact and visibility within your niche.

For those looking to expand their reach and streamline booking processes, speaking bureaus and platforms provide invaluable support. Bureaus like Leading Authorities, American Program Bureau (APB), and BigSpeak Speakers Bureau represent a roster of professional speakers and match them with relevant speaking opportunities. These bureaus handle negotiation, logistics, and contract management, allowing speakers to focus on delivering exceptional presentations.

Moreover, digital platforms such as LinkedIn Events, Eventbrite, and Meetup offer accessible channels for promoting speaking engagements and connecting with potential attendees. By leveraging the power of social media, email marketing, and online communities, speakers can extend their reach and attract a diverse audience to their events. I link to my keynote speaker kit on the "about us" page on my website and from my Linkedin profile.

For me, speaking engagements offer a multifaceted opportunity for individuals and businesses to share expertise, drive impact, and generate income. By strategically positioning yourself as a sought-after speaker, leveraging online resources, and aligning with reputable bureaus and platforms, you can unlock new avenues for visibility, influence, and success in the ever-evolving landscape of public relations.

There can be many opportunities to be asked to be a guest speaker. Below is a list of various places you can consider: Don't forget, your articles can be turned into speeches or workshop topics very quickly.

How to become a TEDx speaker

I'm often asked how to find and get accepted as a TEDx speaker, well here you go.

If you follow these simple steps, then finding TEDx events and getting accepted as a TEDx speaker is virtually guaranteed (if you follow through and put in the effort)

Research TEDx Events: Visit the official TEDx website

(ted.com/tedx) and explore the "Attend" section to find upcoming TEDx events in your area or those you're interested in. You can filter events by location, date, or theme.

Review Event Themes: Each TEDx event has a specific theme or topic. Look for events whose themes align with your expertise, experiences, and the message you want to share. This increases your chances of being selected as a speaker.

Contact Event Organisers: Once you've identified relevant TEDx events, reach out to the organizers expressing your interest in speaking. Introduce yourself, explain why you're passionate about the event's theme, and outline the topic you'd like to present. Provide links to your website, social media profiles, or previous speaking engagements to showcase your credibility.

Prepare a Compelling Proposal: TEDx organisers receive numerous speaker proposals, so it's crucial to make yours stand out. Craft a compelling proposal that clearly articulates your idea worth spreading, its relevance to the event's theme, and why you're the ideal person to deliver it. Include any unique perspectives, personal anecdotes, or innovative approaches that will captivate the audience.

Highlight Your Credentials: Emphasise your expertise, credentials, and relevant accomplishments in your proposal. TEDx organizers look for speakers with diverse backgrounds, unique insights, and compelling stories. Highlight any awards, publications, or notable achievements that demonstrate your authority on the topic.

Practice Your Pitch: Practice delivering your pitch or presentation multiple times to ensure clarity, coherence, and impact. TEDx organizers appreciate speakers who can communicate their ideas effectively and engage the audience with their storytelling abilities.

Follow Submission Guidelines: Pay close attention to the submission guidelines provided by the TEDx event organizers. Ensure your proposal adheres to their requirements regarding format, length, and content. Submit your proposal before the specified deadline to increase your chances of consideration.

Be Persistent and Patient: Securing a speaking opportunity at a TEDx event can be competitive, so be prepared for potential rejections or delays in response. Don't be discouraged by setbacks; instead, continue refining your proposal, seeking feedback, and exploring other TEDx events that align with your interests and expertise.

By following these steps and approaching the process with enthusiasm, authenticity, and perseverance, you can increase your chances of finding TEDx events and getting accepted as a TEDx speaker. Remember to stay true to your passion and purpose, as TEDx events value speakers who have compelling ideas worth sharing with the world.

Which of the following have you researched & approached for a speaking gig?

- Exhibitions (exhibitions.co.uk)
- TED Talk
- Tradeshows / Exhibition / Expo / Summit
- Business Clubs
- Charity Event
- Industry Association
- University / College / School
- TEDx Talk

- Networking Breakfast
- Live Video Networking Event
- Networking Lunch
- Networking Evening Event
- Awards Ceremony
- Chamber of Commerce / Institute
- Cruise ship
- Webcast or Podcast / Guest Panellist
- Live Online Summit

Have you:

- Prepared a Keynote Speaker Kit?
- Created a One Sheet?
- Produced a Showreel or Promotional Video?
- Pre-Engagement Questionnaire?
- Terms & Conditions?

Here's an example of a Keynote Speaker Kit

https://itstacksup.com/wp-content/uploads/2024/02/2024-International-Entrepreneurship-Keynote-Speaker-Kit-Fraser-Hay.pdf

Tell Your Story

Crafting and delivering a captivating keynote from the stage is an art form that leaves an impression on your audience. With a proven template, you can embark on this journey with clarity and confidence. From outlining the narrative arc to refining your delivery techniques, this process ensures that your story resonates deeply with listeners.

Whether you're aiming to inspire, educate, or entertain, effective storytelling can captivate hearts and minds. By honing your skills in planning, writing, and delivery, you'll harness the power of storytelling to leave a memorable impact on your audience. Get ready to step onto the stage and share your story with authenticity and conviction. Use this template & 7 steps to help write your keynote.

Ready?

Step One - Introduction

Either get a 3rd party to introduce yourself using your prepared BIO, online profile, or author profile from Amazon.

If you don't have a prepared Biography or mini CV, then write your ideal introduction.

Step Two – Confirm Interest & Get Permission

After your 3rd party introduction seek to quickly ask 2 questions to engage and involve your audience, and more importantly, to ask their permission to set your agenda and ground rules for the talk. Consider using…

Q. Who wants to [Aim/Objective of key message or talk]?

TIP: Raise your hand and lead your audience

Q. Who would like [offer a benefit or outcome from listening to your talk]?

TIP: Raise your hand and lead your audience

Q. Is it ok that if I ask questions, and for input, you'll engage with me?

TIP: Nod your head and lead your audience

Now think of questions to ask and engage your audience.

Step Three – Where & When

Take the audience back to where and when you want to tell them about the experiences you had.

"I'd like to take you back to...."

"I remember..."

Go on to describe in great detail the scenario or situation that you want to paint for your audience.

Use the space below to describe the scenario you want to share from your past...

Step Four – Challenges

Now you want your audience to agree and/or confirm the challenges they have or are experiencing and how they are the same as to what you experienced back then in step 3.

Hands up if you ever felt…

Stressed by …

frustrated by …

disappointed by…

I worked out that…….

1. Symptom/effects of _____ are often caused by _____

2. Symptom/effects of _____ are often caused by _____

23 Symptom/effects of _____ are often caused by _____

Step 5 – Turning Point

Give examples of what you gained as a direct result of the actions you took. Give personal examples of what you did differently and the results you gained. Be as specific as you can, and use social proof, facts, stats, and evidence.

Explain what you did differently and explain why it helped and what the results were.

1. I used TACTIC #1 - Example 1

2. I used TACTIC #2 - Example 2

3. I used TACTIC #3 - Example 3

4. I used TACTIC #4 - Example 4

Step 6 – What it meant

Here you want to summarise the results, the positive experiences you had and how it felt as a direct result of having taken action and implemented the key tactics as detailed in the previous steps of the process.

You want to list 4 or 5 Key benefits of what it meant to have done what you did, and what the positive outcome(s) were that you achieved.

Step 7 – Call to Action

Summarise your talk, the key points and benefits of your story, your experiences and the actions taken. Then deliver your call to action and what you want your audience to do next. It may include:-

1. Sign up for your "offer."

2. Sign up to your website

3. Sign up to your newsletter

4. Buy your book at the back of the room

5. Post a review of your talk on Facebook, Linkedin etc.

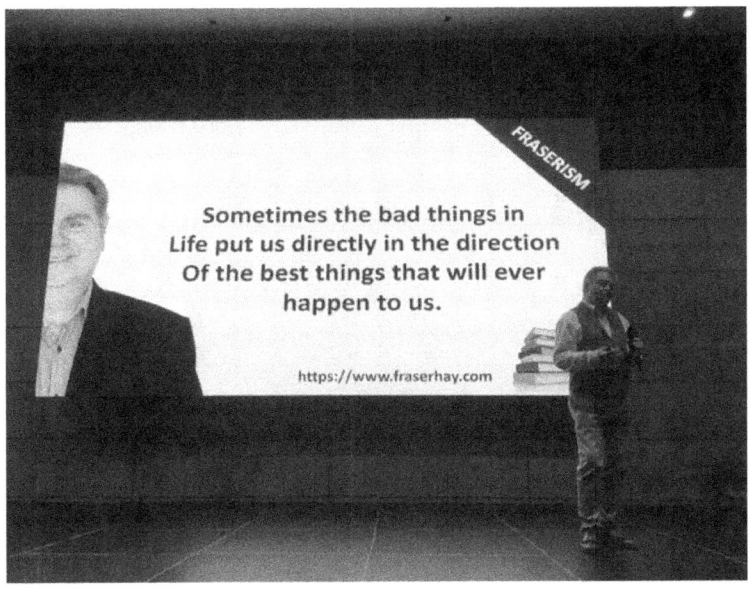

Take a moment to outline how you will deliver your next speaking engagement using the provided template. Reflect on the impact of following a structured process in enhancing your message clarity, audience engagement, and overall effectiveness as a speaker.

Consider how applying this method can elevate your performance and leave a lasting impression on your audience, regardless of the industry or topic. By committing to a systematic approach, you empower yourself to deliver compelling talks that resonate deeply with your listeners and drive meaningful outcomes.

Press Releases

Mastering the art of writing a press release is a vital skill. It's your ticket to getting your message out there, generating buzz, and achieving your PR objectives. A press release serves as your official announcement to the media, informing them about newsworthy events, updates, or initiatives related to your business, organization, or cause.

Imagine you're launching a new product in the tech industry. Crafting a compelling press release can pique the interest of journalists and tech enthusiasts alike, leading to media coverage in leading tech publications like TechCrunch or Wired. Your press release should grab attention from the get-go, with a captivating headline and concise, informative content. It's crucial to convey the significance of your announcement, whether it's a groundbreaking innovation, a partnership with a major player in the industry, or a milestone achievement.

Additionally, consider the audience you're targeting and tailor your press release accordingly. For instance, if you're a nonprofit organisation advocating for environmental sustainability, your press release should highlight the impact of your initiatives on the community and the planet. Aim to strike a balance between information and storytelling, weaving in compelling anecdotes or testimonials to humanize your message.

To enhance your press release writing skills, utilize reaources like online guides, templates, and examples provided by reputable PR organizations such as the Public Relations

Society of America (PRSA) or the Chartered Institute of Public Relations (CIPR). These resources offer valuable insights into best practices, formatting guidelines, and industry trends.

Remember, the goal of a press release is not just to inform but to engage and compel action. Whether it's driving traffic to your website, generating leads, or increasing brand awareness, a well-crafted press release can serve as a powerful tool in your PR arsenal.

By mastering the art of writing press releases, you can effectively communicate your message, attract media attention, and achieve your PR objectives.

Many people have different approaches to writing press releases, and whilst there are thousands of press release distribution services online, you need to ensure that your story is unique, and represents a real reason for the newspaper or other media outlets to want to publish your story.

Is your story timely? Be certain there is some aspect of your news that makes it of interest now, whether it's an event, a new initiative, or a change in your board of directors.

Is your story visual? Many media outlets will want to provide their own photographer or camera crew. For radio, highlight special speakers, authors reading, or background music. However, providing your own pictures can increase the likelihood of getting your "piece" published.

Be aware of deadlines. We've mentioned earlier about lead times and deadlines. Magazine deadlines can be as much as three months before the publication date, television three weeks, weekly publications two to four weeks and daily papers one to two weeks for feature stories or calendar listings.

Consider the news value of your story idea. Will a general audience care about the news you're announcing? Will the media outlet see it as an appropriate story for their readers or viewers? Remember, you must get through the reporter's and editor's "filters."

The following elements should always be included in a news release:

- Contact information—make sure you include a name, phone numbers (office and mobile, if possible), and an email address for the media to contact with questions. (This is different from the phone number provided within the body of the release to be published for the public.)

- Who—include the name of your business, executive directors, quoted sources, speakers, etc.?

- What—the name of the event, a description of the announcement, what your news is about

- When—day of the week, dates, and times (if applicable to your news)

- Where—include the physical address and directions.

- Why—describe the need for the new program or fundraising campaign.

- How—this may include the cost for the public to attend, and how to get tickets if it is an event

- Headline—the title of the release

- Date—the date you are sending the news release.

- Boilerplate—a paragraph at the end of the news release that describes your organization and its mission, ongoing initiatives, and includes the name, location, website, and phone number.

- **Video** – If sending releases out online, you can embed a video for greater impact or to humanise the story and have a company representative make a statement.

- **Resources** – Include one or two links to online website resources.

One Wee press release I wrote got published on over 200 websites including:

Excellent tools to use.

PR Newswire offers comprehensive press release distribution services along with a variety of resources, including press release templates, writing tips, and best practices. Their templates are professionally crafted and customizable to suit various industries and purposes.

HubSpot provides a range of marketing and PR tools, including press release templates and guides. Their templates are user-friendly and designed to help businesses create impactful press releases that resonate with their target audience.

BusinessWire is another reputable press release distribution service that offers a variety of resources for writing effective press releases. Their templates are industry-specific and come with guidelines to ensure your press release meets professional standards.

Cision provides media monitoring and PR solutions, including press release distribution services and templates. Their templates are designed to help businesses craft compelling press releases that capture media attention and drive engagement.

PRWeb offers a range of PR tools and services, including press release templates and writing guides. Their templates are easy to use and come with tips on how to structure and format your press release for maximum impact.

Using these online resources for writing press releases offers several benefits. Firstly, they provide professionally designed templates that save time and effort in creating press releases from scratch.

Secondly, they offer guidance on best practices for writing effective press releases, ensuring your content meets industry standards.

Lastly, these resources often come from reputable PR services, giving your press releases credibility, and increasing their chances of being picked up by media outlets.

Take a moment to outline how you will deliver your next speaking engagement using the provided template. Reflect on the impact of following a structured process in enhancing your message clarity, audience engagement, and overall effectiveness as a speaker.

Consider how applying this method can elevate your performance and leave a lasting impression on your audience, regardless of the industry or topic. By committing to a systematic approach, you empower yourself to deliver compelling talks that resonate deeply with your listeners and drive meaningful outcomes.

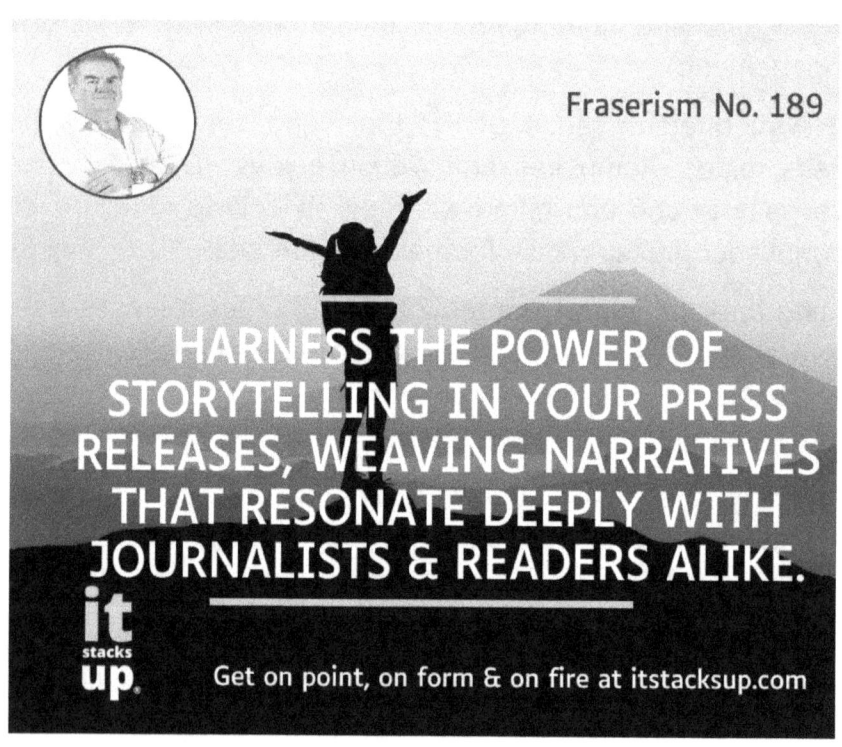

Template Press Release

Feel free to think about how you can personalise the following press release template for it can be a game-changer in effectively communicating your message to the media. o personalizes and use this press release template, follow these simple steps:

1. **Replace** [Your Company Logo], [Company Name], [Address], [City, State, Zip Code], [Phone Number], [Email Address], and [Website] with your company's information.

2. **Modify** [Date] to reflect the current date.

3. **Customize the headline** "Introducing [New Kitchen Widget Name]: Revolutionizing Culinary Creativity for Chefs" with the name of your new kitchen widget.

4. **Update** [City, State] and [Date] to correspond to the location and date of the announcement.

5. **Amend the features listed** under "[New Kitchen Widget Name] offers chefs a range of benefits" with the specific features of your product.

6. **Replace** "[Your Name]" and "[Your Title]" with your name and title within the company.

7. **Adjust** the final paragraph about the free book of soup recipes to match any promotional offer or incentive you're providing.

8. **Lastly, customize** the "About [Company Name]" section with a brief description of your company's background and mission.

9. **Save the press release** with the necessary adjustments and distribute it to relevant media outlets.

This personalized press release will effectively communicate your new kitchen widget launch to the media and target audience, maximizing engagement and coverage.

[Your Company Logo]

[Company Name]

[Address]

[City, State, Zip Code]

[Phone Number]

[Email Address]

[Website]

[Date]

FOR IMMEDIATE RELEASE

Introducing [New Kitchen Widget Name]: Revolutionizing Culinary Creativity for Chefs

[City, State] - [Date] - [Company Name] is thrilled to announce the launch of our latest innovation, [New Kitchen Widget Name], designed to enhance the culinary experience for chefs everywhere. With its innovative features and user-friendly design, [New Kitchen Widget Name] is set to transform the way chefs prepare and create delicious dishes in the kitchen.

[New Kitchen Widget Name] offers chefs a range of benefits, including:

[Feature 1]

[Feature 2]

[Feature 3]

[Feature 4]

"We are excited to introduce [New Kitchen Widget Name] to the culinary world," said [Your Name], [Your Title] at [Company Name]. "Our team has worked tirelessly to develop a product that meets the needs of chefs and empowers them to unleash their creativity in the kitchen."

As part of our launch celebration, we are offering chefs the opportunity to download our free book of soup recipes, curated by our team of culinary experts. This exclusive recipe book is packed with mouthwatering soup recipes that showcase the versatility and capabilities of [New Kitchen Widget Name].

To download your free book of soup recipes and learn more about [New Kitchen Widget Name], visit [Website Link].

About [Company Name]:

[Company Name] is a leading provider of innovative kitchen solutions, dedicated to empowering chefs and culinary enthusiasts to explore their passion for cooking. With a commitment to quality and innovation, we strive to revolutionize the culinary industry one kitchen gadget at a time.

For media inquiries, please contact:

[Your Name]

[Your Title]

[Company Name]

[Phone Number]

[Email Address]

[End of Press Release]

Online Press Releases

In the world of PR, having press releases prepared and knowing where to distribute them online are crucial elements for effective communication and outreach. Take a moment to review your existing press releases. What topics, subjects, issues, or stories do they cover? Are they relevant to your current goals and messaging? Consider the platforms where you plan to post, place, or syndicate your press releases online.

Here are 12 online resources to consider for maximum visibility and reach:

- PRLog.org
- PRWeb.com
- PressBox.co.uk
- Newswire.com
- Merinews.com
- PR-Inside.com
- IndiaPRWire.com
- PR.com
- OpenPR.com
- PowerHomeBiz.com
- ClickPress.com
- 24-7PressRelease.com

Don't underestimate the power of a well-crafted press release and the importance of selecting the right channels for distribution. Invest time in crafting compelling content and utilize these online resources to maximize your PR efforts and achieve your communication goals.

Take a moment to conduct research on your target audience, industry trends, and relevant topics. Identify key messages and compelling angles that will resonate with your audience and capture their attention.

Plan out the structure and content of your press release, ensuring clarity, conciseness, and relevance. Then, write your press release, focusing on engaging headlines and compelling storytelling.

Finally, utilise the online resources provided to distribute your press release to relevant media outlets and platforms. By following these steps diligently, you'll enhance your chances of success in reaching your target audience and achieving your PR objectives.

Other Tools You Can Use

Here are some other tools you can use to help get your message and story out to your intended audience and to help generate exposure,

The Pitch Letter

These days, they're usually sent via email and are crafted to entice a specific reporter with story ideas. Keep it concise, starting with your story concept and why you believe it would interest the reporter and their outlet. Provide a brief background on yourself and your business, and help in conducting research, arranging interviews, and answering queries. Pitch letters are all about selling your story idea and making the journalist's job easier.

Media Alerts

Media alerts are a handy tool to supplement or replace a news release. These succinct, one-page documents outline the details of your event or announcement, including who, what, when, and where, and sometimes why and visual information. They serve as reminders or standalone pieces, particularly useful for simple photo opportunities. Sending them out a day or two before the event ensures journalists are informed and prepared.

Fact Sheets

For quick reference about your organization, fact sheets are indispensable. Typically, one to two pages long, they provide statistical information such as the number of employees or customers, establishment date, website traffic, and more. Fact sheets complement news releases, offering reporters easily accessible data to enhance their stories.

Biographies

Key leaders' biographies, like your CEO or founder, are crucial for speaking engagements and background information for the media. Keep them concise, no more than one page, with details on expertise, education, tenure with the business or industry, relevant experience, and noteworthy community service or interests.

Backgrounder

Background documents offer context about your organisation or specific issues and initiatives. They may include your business's history, location, major awards, or achievements. Background documents provide reporters with comprehensive background information, aiding them in crafting well-informed stories.

FAQs

Frequently Asked Questions (FAQs) are a staple on websites, but they're also invaluable in media materials. They provide accurate, general information and address common queries or misconceptions. Use FAQs to tell your story effectively, tackle objections, and ensure journalists have access to comprehensive information.

By utilizing these PR tools effectively, businesses can enhance their media outreach efforts, provide journalists with valuable resources, and increase their chances of securing media coverage. Whether it's through a compelling pitch letter or a comprehensive backgrounder, strategic use of these materials can elevate your PR strategy and amplify your brand's visibility.

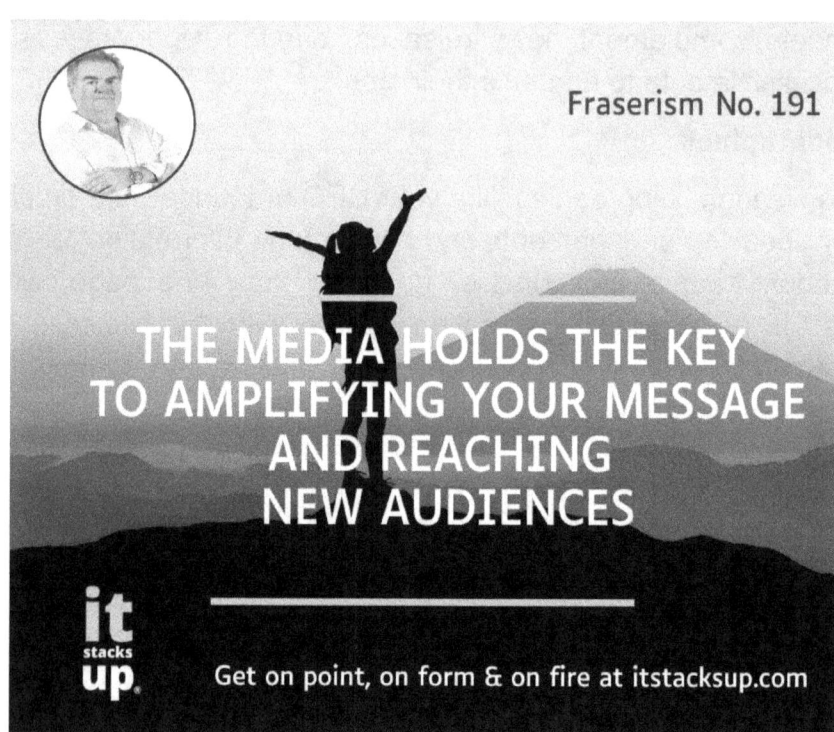

Template Pitch Letter

Often, these are usually sent by email.

From: Fraser J. Hay [mailto:fraser@itstacksup.com]
Sent: Tuesday, June 06, 2022, 2:15 PM
To: XXX@XXXXXXXXX.com
Subject: Entrepreneurship & Marketing Help for small business owners

Hi XXX,

Itstacksup.com wants to help the

- 5.6 million small businesses in the UK

- Generating £4.49 Trillion in 2021

    *Source: Merchantsavvy.co.uk

That have been negatively affected by the Covid-19 Pandemic. Some have seen their entire industry collapse, and many have had to close their doors. Millions of which rely on backlinks, traffic, signups, registrations, leads, enquiries, prospects, sales, and referrals as the lifeblood of their business.

Itstacksup.com has created a membership site with DIY (Do-it-yourself) learning programmes, DWY (Done-With-You) Coaching Programmes and a consultancy offering to help plan, document, automate and execute a marketing strategy.

For future stories, if you'd like a spokesperson or social commentator on entrepreneurship, resilience, social media marketing, business development, MarTech or lead generation and other related issues, please contact me on 01542 663491.

Thank you,

Fraser

Fraser J. Hay

www.itstacksup.com

Template Company Fact Sheet

Instructions: Complete the document below, deleting any section that is not relevant. Ensure your answers are factual, and not full of sales copy. Reporters do want to be "sold."

Headquarters:	**[Enter Company Name]**
	[Enter Street Address]
	[Enter City, County, and Post Code]
	[Enter Phone]
	[Enter Email]
	[Enter URL]
	[Enter contact email address]
Year Founded:	[Enter Year Founded]
Description:	[Enter 50-Word description]
Mission:	[Enter Brand Story]
Products/Services:	[Enter List of Products or Services]
Management	[Enter Names and Titles of Key Management]
Board of Directors:	[Enter Names and Titles of Board of

	Directors, and the company who employ them]
Subsidiaries:	[Enter location and information for subsidiaries]
Awards:	[Enter a list of Awards bestowed upon the company, by whom, and when]
Revenue:	[Enter information about current and previous year's revenues if your company is public]
Significant Achievements:	[Enter a timeline of significant events, product releases, etc.]
Employees:	[Enter # of Employees]
Ownership:	[Enter whether company is privately owned, or publicly held]

Benefits List

Compile a list of Features and Benefits about your products or services and provide answers on this sheet. You could also include this sheet in a Press Kit, Speakers Kit, or include the benefits you create on a sales page for your products/services.

F: **[Enter Feature]**

B: which means [Enter Benefit]

F: **[Enter Feature]**

B: which means [Enter Benefit]

F: **[Enter Feature]**

B: which means [Enter Benefit]

F: **[Enter Feature]**

B: which means [Enter Benefit]

F: **[Enter Feature]**

B: which means [Enter Benefit]

F: **[Enter Feature]**

B: which means [Enter Benefit]

F: **[Enter Feature]**

B: which means [Enter Benefit]

F: **[Enter Feature]**

B: which means [Enter Benefit]

F: **[Enter Feature]**

B: which means [Enter Benefit]

Facts & Bullet Points

Think about all the different and amazing facts about your marketplace, your products, service, business, and track record. You want to be able to demonstrate you are an expert in your field. Create a list of 10 facts in each category.

Marketplace Facts (Your facts should demonstrate that you know your market)

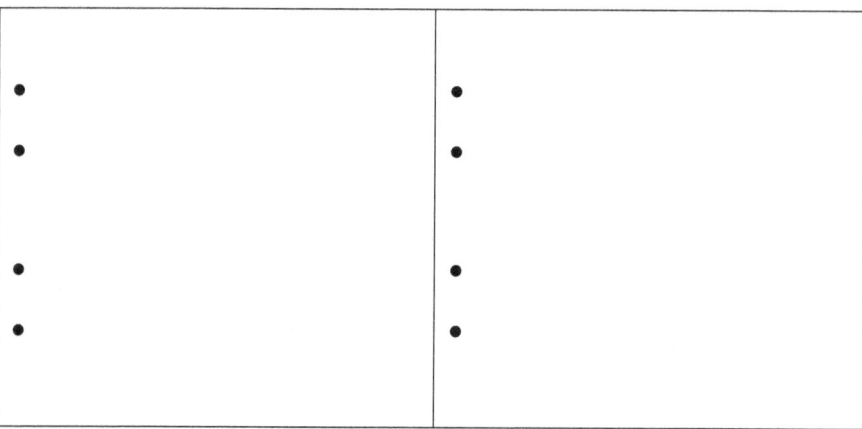

Your Products (Your facts should demonstrate your product knowledge)

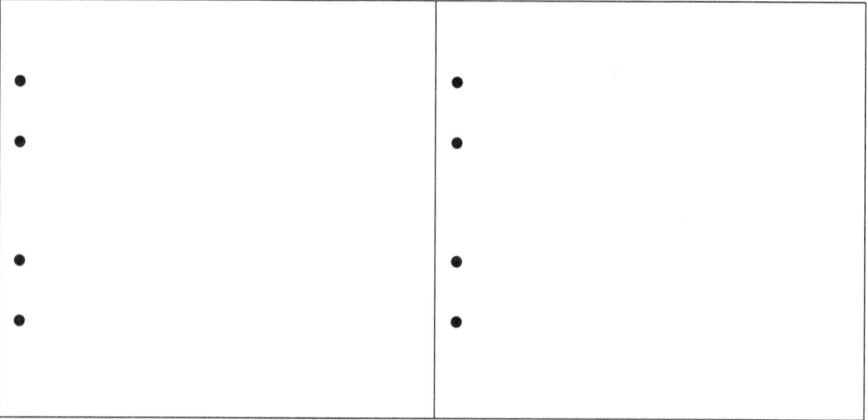

Your Business / yourself (List achievements, accolades, awards etc.)

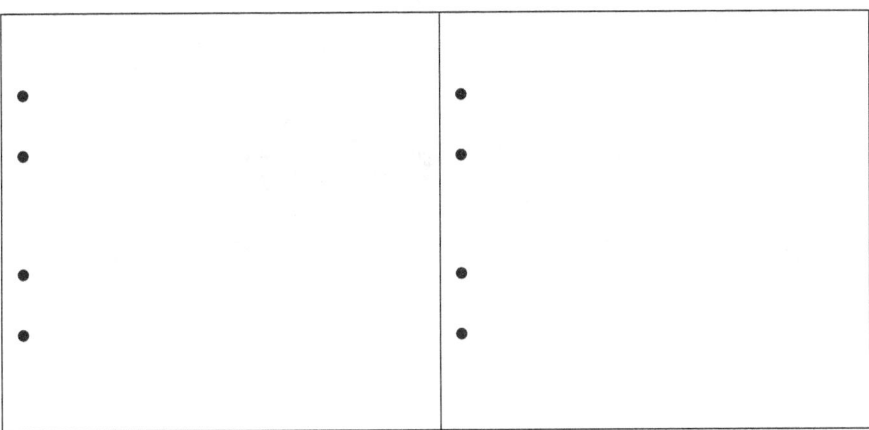

•	•
•	•
•	•
•	•

Your Competitors (List facts that without being too negative about them)

•	•
•	•
•	•
•	•

Now reduce the size of each list, from ten down to your best five

 Take time to think about all the amazing facts you can share with journalists and your audience. Complete the above exercise and make a list of 10 – 30 facts that are interesting, intriguing, or very surprising.

Case Study Template TELATE

Insert a one or two sentence company description of your customer or client here. Summarize what your company did for this customer and your results. Provide as much detail as you can. Remember, people love facts and numbers!

Industry:

[Client Industry #1]

Project Type [or Product Name]:

[Product #1], [Product #2], and [Product #3]

Challenge

[Insert copy in this section that explains why the company needed the solution and your company's products/services. What problem was your customer looking to solve? Keep this   to 3-5 sentences.]

Solution

[Insert what your corganisation did to solve this challenge. What did you provide to create a solution? Explain how you personalized or customized the solution for the customer's particular scenario.]

Results

[Insert copy here that really highlights how your solution has helped this customer. Share what you reduced or eliminated. Share what you increased or improved for the customer. The more specific you can be in terms of the results that you generated – the better. Demonstrate why people will want to seek you out.]

Customer Feedback

[*Insert a positive quote from the customer here. It doesn't need to be longer than a sentence.*]

 Ensure you take notes and reflect on the above. Discuss the points with other members of your team. Have you completed the exercise above?

0. Not Applicable.

1. Yes. All done & documented.

2. On the case. Working towards it, documenting it.

3. Oops. No, not yet completed (or started).

4. This is all too overwhelming. I Need help with this – fast.

Template Biography (BIO) Questionnaire

Answer the following questions to complete a Bio page for your press kit, speakers kit or About Us part of your website. It is useful for having a Bio prepared for press interviews or to give seminar or workshop hosts that have asked you to speak on a particular topic or subject. The answers you give should enable you to create a One-page Bio.

1. **What is Your Name?**

2. **What is Your Position Within the Business?**

3. **What Year Did You Join (or Start) The business?**

4. **What is Your Role & Responsibilities Within the Business?**

5. Have You Held Other Positions Previously, Within the Business? If so, What Were the Roles & Responsibilities?

6. Please Provide a Brief Work History, The Roles & Responsibilities with Each Employer...

7. What is Your Educational Background?

8. Do You Belong to Any Associations or Trade Bodies?

9. Have You Published Any Books or Whitepapers? Where?

10.Have You Delivered a TED Talk or TEDX Talk?

Ensure you take notes and reflect on the above. Discuss the points with other members of your team. Have you completed the exercise above?

0. Not Applicable.

1. Yes. All done & documented.

2. On the case. Working towards it, documenting it.

3. Oops. No, not yet completed (or started).

4. This is all too overwhelming. I Need help with this – fast.

FAQs

Compile a list of questions asked by Clients, Partners, Staff or Journalists about your products and services, and provide answers on this sheet. You could also include this sheet in a Press Kit, Speakers Kit, or to create an FAQ page on your website. You could also use it as the basis for interviews with journalists and presenters.

TIP: By preparing the questions journalists will ask you, can help to present you in a particularly good light.

Q: **[Enter Question]?**

A: [Enter Answer]

Q: **[Enter Question]?**

A: [Enter Answer]

Q: **[Enter Question]?**

A: [Enter Answer]

Q: **[Enter Question]?**

A: [Enter Answer]

Q: **[Enter Question]?**

A: [Enter Answer]

    Ensure you take notes and reflect on the above. Discuss the points with other members of your team. Have you completed the exercise above?

0. Not Applicable.

1. Yes. All done & documented.

2. On the case. Working towards it, documenting it.

3. Oops. No, not yet completed (or started).

4. This is all too overwhelming. I Need help with this – fast.

Dealing With the Press

When it comes to dealing with the press, preparation is key to success. Following simple yet practical guidelines can make all the difference in how you are perceived and the coverage you receive. One of the main reasons preparations are crucial is because journalists often work on tight deadlines and expect concise and relevant information. By being prepared, you not only save their time but also increase the likelihood of your story being picked up.

For example, imagine you're launching a new product and want media coverage. If you're well-prepared with a press release containing all the necessary details, photos, and quotes, journalists are more likely to include your story in their publication. On the other hand, if you're disorganized and fail to provide the required information promptly, you may miss valuable coverage opportunities.

Moreover, being prepared instills confidence and professionalism, both of which are essential when dealing with the press. By following simple guidelines such as being clear, concise, and responsive, you can ensure a positive interaction with journalists and increase your chances of achieving your PR objectives.

Interview Do's and Don'ts

Do's

- Ask the reporter what will be covered in the interview so you (or the appropriate person) can be prepared.

- Know the points you want to make before your interview. What are your two or three key messages? Make sure you get them across early and often.

- Use the inverted pyramid technique in phrasing your statements and responses—make the most important point first.

- Do your homework. Read stories by the reporter or watch interviewer's technique with other guests (if television) before your interview or appearance.

- Use positive body language. Lean forward, make eye contact, and use your hands to gesture.

- For TV, ensure you use short sound bites. (Ones that can be recorded.)

- Make sure you understand a question before you answer.

- If you can't answer a question, explain why (briefly). If it's a print interview, find the information and get back to the reporter by their deadline.

Don'ts

- Don't engage in an argument.

- Don't use profanity, professional jargon, or make jokes.

- Don't speak off the record. Never say anything you don't want to appear in print or on the air.

- Don't speak from opinion—you are your organisation's spokesperson.

- Never say "no comment."

Fraserism No. 192

AUTHENTICITY IS THE CORNERSTONE OF GENUINE CONNECTION, ALLOWING US TO EMBRACE OUR TRUE SELVES

it stacks up.

Get on point, on form & on fire at itstacksup.com

Interview Techniques

Whether you're representing yourself, your business, or a cause, the way you handle press interactions can significantly impact your reputation and the outcome of the coverage you receive.

Without a doubt, preparation is key to ensuring that you convey your message effectively and accurately. Imagine being interviewed by a journalist about a recent business initiative. By preparing in advance with key talking points, relevant data, and compelling anecdotes, you can ensure that your message is clear, concise, and impactful. For example, if you're launching a new sustainability initiative, having statistics on carbon emissions reduction and success stories from customers or employees can help illustrate the importance and impact of your efforts.

Moreover, good interview techniques can help you navigate challenging questions and maintain control of the conversation. Techniques such as active listening, staying on message, and bridging to key points can help you address questions confidently while steering the conversation back to your intended message. For instance, if a journalist asks about a recent controversy, acknowledging the issue briefly before pivoting to discuss the steps your organization is taking to address it demonstrates transparency and accountability while keeping the focus on positive actions.

Following practical guidelines is also essential for ensuring successful media interaction. This includes being punctual, respectful, and responsive to journalists' inquiries. For instance, if a reporter reaches out for comments on a breaking news story, responding promptly and offering relevant insights can position you as a reliable source and increase the likelihood of your comments being included in their coverage.

Additionally, understanding the nuances of different media formats and audiences is crucial for tailoring your message effectively. For example, a live television interview requires concise and engaging responses, while a print article may allow for more detailed explanations. By adapting your communication style and content to suit the specific medium, you can maximize the impact of your message and reach a broader audience.

For me, being prepared with good interview techniques and following practical guidelines is essential for successful media interactions. By taking the time to prepare, hone your communication skills, and adhere to best practices, you can ensure that your message resonates with journalists and audiences alike, enhancing your reputation and achieving your PR objectives.

One of the most effective techniques that interviewees can use to help retain control of an interview is called "bridging." Verbal bridges allow an interviewee:

1. To steer a reporter back to relevant topics and key messages that they want to convey.

2. To move away from controversial, uncomfortable, or unflattering topics and back on to key messages.

3. Complete each answer to each question with a prepared sound bite.

Bridging Techniques

When used appropriately, the following "bridges" can serve as effective tools of verbal control and defense:

- "Whilst not my area of expertise, I do think your audience would be interested in knowing that . . . "

- "Let me just add that . . . "

- "That reminds me . . . "

- "Let me answer you by saying that . . . "

- "That's an important point because . . . "

- "What that means is . . ."

- "Another thing to remember is . . . "

- "If you look at it closely, you'll find . . . "

- "I don't know. But what I do know is . . . "

Flagging Techniques

You can give the reporter verbal clues about important comments so that you can stress key elements in your message.

- The most important point here is …

- The underlying cause …

- The goal is …

- The real issue is…

Hooking Techniques

You can let reporters know upfront you have several points to make, and you can use this technique to maneuver the discussion where you want. Also, it lets the listener know you have several elements to cover.

- The first of the three elements involved in this issue…

- There are two primary rationales…

- We really have three important reasons for pursuing…

Crisis management, at its best, is crisis avoidance.

Crisis avoidance involves excellent issues management.

Issues Management Management

Issues management is a critical aspect of any organization's public relations strategy, particularly when dealing with the press. It involves identifying, addressing, and mitigating potential challenges or controversies that may arise and could negatively impact the organization's reputation or operations. In today's fast-paced and interconnected world, where news travels rapidly and public scrutiny is heightened, effective issues management is essential for maintaining trust and credibility.

One key reason issues management is important is its role in preserving reputation and brand image. Consider a scenario where a consumer goods company faces allegations of using unethical labor practices in its supply chain. Without a proactive approach to address these allegations and communicate transparently with stakeholders, the company risks significant damage to its reputation and consumer trust. By promptly acknowledging the issue, conducting thorough investigations, and implementing corrective actions, the company can demonstrate accountability and commitment to ethical standards, thereby mitigating reputational harm.

Issues management can enable organisations to navigate complex and sensitive issues with stakeholders, including the media, government agencies, and advocacy groups. For example, a pharmaceutical company may encounter public concerns regarding the safety or efficacy of its products. By engaging in proactive communication, providing accurate information, and addressing concerns in a timely manner, the company can foster trust and credibility among regulators, healthcare professionals, and consumers, safeguarding its market position and reputation.

Being prepared is paramount when managing issues in the press. This involves establishing clear protocols, designated spokespersons, and communication channels to ensure a coordinated and effective response. For example, a cybersecurity firm experiencing a data breach must have a comprehensive crisis communication plan in place, outlining steps for notifying affected parties, coordinating with law enforcement, and managing media inquiries. By proactively preparing for potential crises and equipping spokespersons with media training, organizations can respond swiftly and decisively, minimizing reputational damage and restoring stakeholder confidence.

In addition to proactive measures, it's essential to monitor media coverage and public sentiment to identify emerging issues and trends. By leveraging media monitoring tools and social listening platforms, organizations can stay informed about potential reputational risks and take preemptive action to address them. For instance, a financial services company may use sentiment analysis to track online discussions about customer satisfaction and promptly address any negative feedback to prevent reputational damage.

For me, issues management plays a vital role in safeguarding reputation, maintaining stakeholder trust, and navigating complex challenges in the press. By adopting a proactive and strategic approach, organizations can effectively manage issues, mitigate risks, and protect their brand integrity in an increasingly dynamic and competitive media landscape.

What the experts say

Effective issues and crisis management is essential for any

organization to protect its reputation and maintain stakeholder trust. By proactively identifying potential issues and implementing strategies to address them, companies can mitigate risks and minimise the impact of crises when they arise.

As Warren Buffett famously said, *'It takes 20 years to build a reputation and five minutes to ruin it. If you think about that, you'll do things differently.'* This quote underscores the importance of proactive reputation management and the need for organizations to be prepared for unforeseen challenges. Source: Warren Buffett, Chairman and CEO of Berkshire Hathaway.

Issues management is the wide scope of activities that can help an organisation

manage issues which, if not effectively managed, could become a crisis. Good issues management creates a wall of protection, or a cushion, in times of crisis.

Communications in times of crisis are credible only if you already have a cushion of credibility from quality, believable, and reliable issues management communications prior to the crisis. Your actions must be consistent with your words.

The most fundamental component of issues management is a clear, consistent message.

First, be clear what your message is intended to accomplish.

Effective messages are spoken in the language of the listener; in other words, the message means something to the person with whom you are communicating. Present information in terms of benefits to the listener. Don't just flash tons of features that may or may not click with the listener and only have meaning for you.

Memorable messages must include one or more of the following elements (know your audience when using any of the following):

- Light humour and for issues management only. Be warned, though, what is funny to you may not be funny to someone else. Humor should **not** be used in crisis communications.

- Alliteration

- Play on words (Again, for crisis messages, this is unlikely to be well received. But it is useful in issue management.)

- Emotionally charged words

- Repetition

Memorable and effective messages also should fall under one of the following categories:

- Logic & Authenticity

- Action-oriented

- Believable

- Measurable

- Strikes a nerve.

- Timely

- Visionary

Effective messages are delivered clearly, directly, and empathetically. Never be condescending. Professional assistance with message development and media training is a prudent investment. People who know the most about an issue often find it the most difficult to create an effective message. Helpful hints:

- Determine what is the most important piece of information.

- Ask yourself, who cares? Why do they care?

- How does the message fit into your overall branding?

Crisis ManagementIssues

Every organisation, regardless of size or industry, is vulnerable to crises that can emerge from various sources—be it product recalls, financial scandals, natural disasters, or public relations missteps. Effective crisis management not only enables companies to weather the storm but also presents opportunities to emerge stronger and more trusted than before.

Consider the case of Johnson & Johnson in 1982 when cyanide-laced Tylenol capsules led to multiple deaths, threatening the company's reputation and financial stability. Through swift action, transparent communication, and a bold decision to recall all Tylenol products nationwide, Johnson & Johnson demonstrated exemplary crisis management. By prioritizing consumer safety and taking responsibility, the company not only salvaged its brand but also set a new standard for corporate crisis response.

Another compelling example is the 2010 BP Deepwater Horizon oil spill, one of the most catastrophic environmental disasters in history. BP faced intense public scrutiny and legal repercussions as the spill wreaked havoc on marine life and coastal communities. Despite initial missteps in communication and containment efforts, BP eventually implemented comprehensive crisis management measures. By accepting accountability, allocating resources for cleanup and compensation, and implementing stricter safety protocols, BP managed to restore some public trust and mitigate long-term damage to its brand.

These examples underscore the importance of proactive crisis management in mitigating the impact of adverse events and preserving organizational reputation. By promptly addressing crises, organizations can demonstrate their commitment to stakeholders, uphold transparency, and maintain credibility even in the face of adversity.

On thing is for sure, effective crisis management can yield favorable outcomes, fostering resilience and enabling companies to emerge stronger post-crisis. In the aftermath of the 2015 E. coli outbreak linked to its food products, Chipotle Mexican Grill implemented rigorous food safety protocols and launched a comprehensive marketing campaign to rebuild consumer trust. Despite facing significant financial losses and negative publicity, Chipotle's proactive crisis response contributed to its eventual recovery and reaffirmed its commitment to food safety.

Conversely, mishandling crises can lead to irreparable damage, tarnished reputations, and even business failure. In 2017, United Airlines faced a public relations nightmare when a video of a passenger being forcibly removed from an overbooked flight went viral. United's initial response was widely criticized as insensitive and defensive, exacerbating public outrage, and damaging the airline's image. The incident served as a cautionary tale of the consequences of poor crisis management, resulting in a significant decline in customer trust and brand perception.

To navigate crises effectively, organizations must adopt a proactive and strategic approach to crisis management. This entails establishing clear protocols, designated crisis response teams, and robust communication channels to facilitate timely and coordinated actions. Training key personnel in crisis response and media relations is also essential to ensure a unified and coherent message during turbulent times.

Furthermore, leveraging technology and social media monitoring tools can provide valuable insights into emerging threats and public sentiment, enabling organizations to anticipate and address issues before they escalate into full-blown crises. Platforms like Brandwatch and Hootsuite allow companies to monitor online conversations, identify potential crises, and engage with stakeholders in real time, enhancing crisis preparedness and response capabilities.

For me, crisis management is an indispensable aspect of modern business strategy, essential for protecting reputation, maintaining stakeholder trust, and preserving organizational resilience. By learning from past examples, implementing proactive measures, and embracing transparency and accountability, organizations can navigate crises effectively and emerge stronger from adversity. As the saying goes, *"In the midst of chaos, there is also opportunity"*—a testament to the transformative power of effective crisis management.

The 10 Commandments of Crisis Management

In the tumultuous realm of crisis communications, adherence to the "10 Commandments" can spell the difference between reputation redemption and irreparable damage. Let's dissect these commandments with real-life examples to illuminate their significance:

Meeting the storm head-on was exemplified by Johnson & Johnson during the Tylenol poisoning crisis in 1982. Instead of evading responsibility, they swiftly recalled all products, prioritizing public safety over profit.

The cardinal sin of saying "no comment" was committed by British Petroleum (BP) during the Deepwater Horizon oil spill. Their lack of transparency fueled public outrage and eroded trust.

United Airlines learned the hard way that hiding from reporters amplifies negative publicity. The mishandling of the passenger removal incident in 2017 led to widespread condemnation and a PR nightmare.

Speaking off the record can backfire spectacularly, as evidenced by former US President Richard Nixon during the Watergate scandal. His clandestine remarks were exposed, leading to his eventual resignation.

The importance of preparation was underscored by Chipotle Mexican Grill after a string of food safety incidents. By implementing robust crisis plans and proactive measures, they regained consumer trust and loyalty.

Bearing false witness can irreparably damage credibility, as seen in the case of Volkswagen's emission scandal. Their deceitful practices resulted in hefty fines and tarnished the brand reputation.

Showing anger in crisis situations, as demonstrated by BP's former CEO Tony Hayward, only exacerbates public outrage, and diminishes empathy.

Honouring other people's emotions is crucial, as demonstrated by Starbucks' response to a racial bias incident in one of its stores. Their swift action and genuine apology resonated with stakeholders and fostered reconciliation.

Repetition of the message is vital for clarity and consistency, as exemplified by Apple during product recalls. Their transparent communication and regular updates reassured customers and mitigated backlash.

Showing genuine empathy, as displayed by Airbnb after a host discrimination incident, builds trust and fosters goodwill. Their commitment to diversity and inclusion resonated positively with stakeholders.

These should serve as guiding principles for effective crisis communication, emphasizing transparency, empathy, and accountability. By heeding these commandments and learning from past mistakes, organizations can navigate crises with integrity.

Take a moment, to imagine yourself in a hypothetical scenario where your organization is facing a significant crisis. Consider the emotions you would experience, such as fear, uncertainty, and pressure.

Then, brainstorm potential strategies and actions you could take to address the crisis effectively, keeping in mind the impact on various stakeholders and the reputation of your organization.

By engaging in this exercise, you'll gain a deeper understanding of the importance of proactive crisis management in safeguarding your organization's brand and fostering trust among stakeholders.

Risk Assessment

The first step in crisis management is risk assessment, or vulnerability audit. This evaluation is best conducted with the assistance of professionals who guide you through various "what-if" scenarios, but the assessments can be conducted in-house.

An important contraindication for in-house assessments is participant willingness to speak freely, confidentially, and honestly with the reviewer. This is critical because some of the most destructive crises are not natural disasters or accidents but those that smolder within an organization until they flare up and escape into the public consciousness.

These crises can include discrimination or harassment charges, embezzlement, and theft, "accepted" breaking of health and safety rules, employment issues, alleged criminal charges such as fraud etc.

An example of Risk Assessment Questionnaire

Identification of Potential Risks:

- Are you aware of any potential risks or issues that could negatively impact your organization's reputation or brand image?

- Have you experienced any past incidents that have caused reputational harm or public scrutiny?

Stakeholder Analysis:

- Who are your key stakeholders, including customers, employees, shareholders, and the community?

- How might potential risks or crises affect each stakeholder group?

Media and Public Perception:

- How do you perceive your organization's current public image and reputation?
- Are there any negative perceptions or misconceptions that need to be addressed?

Industry and Regulatory Environment:

- Are there any industry-specific regulations or standards that could impact your organization's operations or reputation?
- How do changes in the regulatory environment affect your risk exposure?

Internal Communication and Preparedness:

- Do you have clear communication channels and protocols in place for managing crises internally?
- Are key stakeholders within your organization aware of their roles and responsibilities in the event of a crisis?

External Communication Strategy:

- Do you have a crisis communication plan in place to effectively manage external communication during a crisis?
- Have you identified spokespersons and designated media contacts for handling inquiries from the press and public?

Monitoring and Response Mechanisms:

- How do you monitor and assess potential risks and threats to your organisation's reputation?

- What measures are in place to enable swift and effective response to crises as they arise?

Scenario Planning and Simulation Exercises:

- Have you conducted scenario planning exercises to anticipate potential crises and test your organization's response capabilities?

- How frequently do you review and update your crisis management plans based on lessons learned from past incidents or industry trends?

Resource Allocation and Budgeting:

- Do you allocate sufficient resources and budget for crisis preparedness and response activities?

- How do you prioritize investments in risk management initiatives based on the likelihood and potential impact of identified risks?

Continuous Improvement and Learning:

- Do you conduct post-mortem analyses following crises to identify areas for improvement and enhance your organization's resilience?

- Are you committed to ongoing learning and professional development in the field of crisis management and reputation risk?

Create "Placeholder" Statements

A placeholder statement serves as a pre-drafted response or set of responses formulated and approved by you and your team in advance of a crisis. In moments of crisis, relying solely on memory may result in inconsistencies or errors in communication. Therefore, having predefined statements allows other team members to effectively address inquiries or comments related to specific issues, even in the absence of key personnel.

For example, in the healthcare industry, a placeholder statement addressing patient safety concerns could be: "Ensuring the safety and well-being of our patients is our top priority. We are currently investigating the matter and will provide updates as soon as more information becomes available." Similarly, in the technology sector, a statement addressing a data breach might be: "Protecting the privacy and security of our users' data is paramount. We are working diligently to address the situation and will take necessary measures to mitigate any potential risks."

Other Industry specific examples.

Product Recall in the Food Industry. "The safety and well-being of our consumers is our utmost priority. We are actively investigating reports of [specific issue] and are committed to resolving it swiftly. Our customers can rest assured that we are taking all necessary steps to address the situation and prevent any further risks. We will provide updates as soon as new information becomes available."

Data Breach in a Tech Company. "Protecting the privacy and security of our users' data is fundamental to our business. We are currently investigating a potential data breach and are working diligently to assess the extent of the incident. Our team is taking immediate action to contain the breach and enhance our security measures. We understand the concern this may cause and assure our users that we are committed to transparency and will provide updates throughout the investigation."

Workplace Safety Incident in a Manufacturing Plant. "The safety and well-being of our employees are of paramount importance to us. We are deeply saddened by the incident that occurred at our facility today. Our priority is to ensure the affected individuals receive the necessary medical attention and support. We are cooperating fully with the relevant authorities in their investigation. Rest assured; we are reviewing our safety protocols to prevent such incidents in the future. Our thoughts are with those affected by this unfortunate event."

Environmental Impact Incident in an Energy Company. "We are aware of the concerns regarding [specific environmental issue] associated with our operations. As a company committed to environmental stewardship, we take these concerns seriously. We are actively investigating the situation and are working closely with environmental agencies to assess and address the impact. Our goal is to mitigate any environmental damage and implement measures to prevent similar incidents in the future. We remain dedicated to transparent communication and will provide updates as our investigation progresses."

By categorising potential crises and preparing corresponding placeholder statements, organizations can ensure a prompt and consistent response to various issues that may arise. Additionally, assigning individuals to monitor relevant events across different media channels, including traditional and online platforms, enables proactive management of emerging situations, safeguarding the organization's reputation, and maintaining stakeholder trust.

Possible Crises that you may wish to prepare for

- Product recall due to safety concerns
- Data breach compromising customer information.
- Executive misconduct allegations

- Negative media coverage regarding environmental practices
- Workplace accidents resulting in injuries or fatalities.
- Financial fraud or accounting irregularities
- Cybersecurity breach affecting business operations.
- Defective product causing harm to consumers.
- Legal disputes or litigation involving the company.
- Employee strikes or labor disputes
- Supply chain disruptions impacting product availability.
- Public health crisis related to product contamination.
- Social media backlash over controversial marketing campaigns
- Natural disasters affecting business operations.
- Negative customer reviews or social media posts damaging reputation
- _____
- _____

Take a moment to imagine yourself in a hypothetical scenario where your organisation is facing a significant crisis. Consider the emotions you would experience, such as fear, uncertainty, and pressure.

Then, brainstorm potential strategies and actions you could take to address the crisis effectively, keeping in mind the impact on various stakeholders and the reputation of your organization.

By engaging in this exercise, you'll gain a deeper understanding of the importance of proactive crisis management in safeguarding your organization's brand and fostering trust among stakeholders.

Fraserism No. 194

RISK IS THE BRIDGE TO
OPPORTUNITY;
DARE TO CROSS IT.

Get on point, on form & on fire at itstacksup.com

Listening to and monitoring the "Buzz"

As part of your online PR Campaign, you need to tap into the **online conversation** to in the realm of PR, harnessing the power of online conversations is paramount to understanding the pulse of your audience, competitors, and industry. Monitoring the digital buzz surrounding your brand, products, and peers can unveil valuable insights that guide your PR strategies. To effectively gauge the sentiment, identify influencers, and stay abreast of key issues, employing various online tools is indispensable. Here's a curated list of 14 resources to aid in social monitoring and listening:

- **Google Alerts:** Receive email notifications for specific keywords or topics online.
- **Blogpulse: Track** trends and conversations across the blogosphere.
- **How Sociable:** Evaluate your brand's social media presence and impact.
- **Answerthepublic:** Discover common questions and concerns in your industry.
- **DataEQ:** Harness data analytics to understand online sentiments and trends.
- **Brainsight:** Visualize social media conversations and trends for deeper analysis.
- **Survey Sparrow:** Gather feedback and insights through customizable surveys.
- **Net Vibes:** Create custom dashboards to monitor social media, news & RSS feeds.

- **Ubfluence:** Identify and engage with social media influencers to amplify your message.
- **Qualtrics:** Conduct comprehensive market research and sentiment analysis.
- **Amazon:** Monitor customer reviews and ratings for products and services.
- **Trust Pilot:** Track and manage online reviews and reputation.
- **Google Trends:** Explore search trends and topics relevant to your industry.

By leveraging these tools, PR professionals can answer critical questions about their brand, competitors, and industry, such as:

- What is the sentiment surrounding our brand and products?
- How do our competitors fare in terms of online reputation?
- What are the prevailing topics and issues within our industry?
- What are customers saying about the latest authors and books in our domain?
- What emerging trends should we be aware of and capitalize on?

Monitoring online conversations and social trends not only allows PR practitioners to stay informed but also enables them to adapt their strategies in real-time, ensuring they remain relevant and responsive in today's dynamic digital landscape. Ask yourself the following questions:

What is "Buzz" about you and your products and is it Positive or Negative?

_____

_____

_____

What is the "Buzz" about your competitors and is it Positive or Negative?

_____

_____

_____

What is the "Buzz" in your industry and is it Positive or Negative?

_____

_____

_____

What is the "Buzz" regarding the latest authors & books in your "space" - is it Positive or Negative?

_____

_____

_____

Other tools and resources you may find useful:

Followerwonk: Analyses Twitter followers, identifies influencers, and measures.

engagement to optimize social media strategies.

Trendspottr: Predicts emerging trends and viral content on social media to stay ahead of the curve.

Trackur: Monitors brand mentions, analyzes sentiment, and measures social media engagement to improve brand reputation.

Synthesio: Tracks social media conversations, measures sentiment, and analyzes audience demographics to inform marketing strategies.

Zoho Social: Manages social media accounts, schedules posts, analyzes engagement metrics, and tracks brand mentions in real-time.

CrowdTangle: Monitors social media content, tracks engagement, and identifies viral trends to optimize content strategy.

Rignite: Manages social media campaigns, schedules posts, analyzes performance metrics, and tracks brand mentions across platforms.

Nuvi: Provides real-time social media monitoring, sentiment analysis, and competitive benchmarking to enhance brand visibility.

Digimind: Monitors social media conversations, tracks brand sentiment, and analyzes audience behavior to inform marketing decisions.

Klear: Identifies social media influencers, measures audience engagement, and analyzes competitor performance to optimize social strategies.

Union Metrics: Analyzes social media content, measures engagement, and provides actionable insights to improve campaign performance.

Sysomos Heartbeat: Monitors social media conversations, tracks brand sentiment, and measures share of voice to gauge brand reputation.

Zignal Labs: Analyzes real-time data from social media, news, and broadcast sources to track brand mentions and measure campaign impact.

Sprinklr: Manages social media channels, analyzes audience sentiment, and measures campaign performance to optimize social strategies.

These resources offer benefits such as real-time monitoring, sentiment analysis, influencer identification, campaign management, and competitive benchmarking, helping businesses effectively manage their social media presence and improve brand visibility.

Take a moment to conduct a social media audit for your organisation. Use monitoring tools like Mention or Hootsuite to track brand mentions, sentiment, and engagement across various social media platforms.

Pay attention to the tone of conversations, identify key influencers, and note any emerging trends or issues. Analyze the data to gain insights into your audience's perceptions and preferences and use this information to refine your PR strategy.

By actively listening to your audience and monitoring their feedback, you can better understand their needs and expectations, enhancing your PR efforts and driving meaningful results.

Establish Your Share of Voice

Determining your share of voice in PR is crucial for understanding your brand's visibility and influence within your industry or market. Share of voice refers to the percentage of the overall conversation or media coverage that your brand occupies compared to competitors or other relevant entities. This metric provides valuable insights into your brand's presence and impact in the public sphere. By analysing your share of voice, you can gauge the effectiveness of your PR efforts, identify areas for improvement, and benchmark against competitors.

One of the key reasons why determining your share of voice is important is that it allows you to assess your brand's performance relative to competitors. By comparing your share of voice to that of competitors, you can evaluate whether your PR activities are helping you gain traction and visibility or if you're being overshadowed by others in your industry. For example, if your share of voice is significantly lower than that of a competitor, it may indicate that you need to ramp up your PR efforts to increase your brand's visibility and relevance.

Additionally, determining your share of voice helps you track your progress over time and measure the success of your PR campaigns. By regularly monitoring changes in your share of voice, you can assess the impact of specific PR initiatives, such as media outreach, content marketing, or event participation. For example, if you see a significant increase in your share of voice following a product launch or media tour, it suggests that your efforts are resonating with your target audience and generating buzz around your brand.

Brandwatch offers comprehensive social listening and analytics tools that allow businesses to measure their share of voice across various online channels. It provides insights into brand mentions, sentiment analysis, and competitive benchmarking. By analysing social media conversations and online mentions, Brandwatch helps businesses understand their market presence and performance relative to competitors, enabling informed decision-making and effective strategy development.

Of all the different conversations that exist online about you, your competitors, your I

ndustry etc. what % share of voice do you have? Are you actively participating in the same channels, and communities as your clients, suppliers, peers, and competitors, and if so, how much are you helping to shape what's going on? Are you a leader, a lurker, or a hanger on? Are people talking about topics, or you, specifically? Remember,

share of voice leads to market share. The most trusted form of advertising is now "conversation," or more specifically a conversation about an experience with your brand – Own it.

_____

_____

_____

_____

_____

 Take a moment to conduct a share of voice analysis for your brand or organization. Start by identifying your key competitors and relevant industry players.

Then, use online monitoring tools to track and compare the volume and sentiment of mentions across different channels, such as social media, news articles, and blogs.

Pay attention to the topics and themes associated with your brand and competitors, as well as the overall tone of the conversation. By gaining insights into your share of voice, you can better understand your competitive landscape, identify areas for improvement, and refine your PR strategy to enhance your brand's visibility and influence.

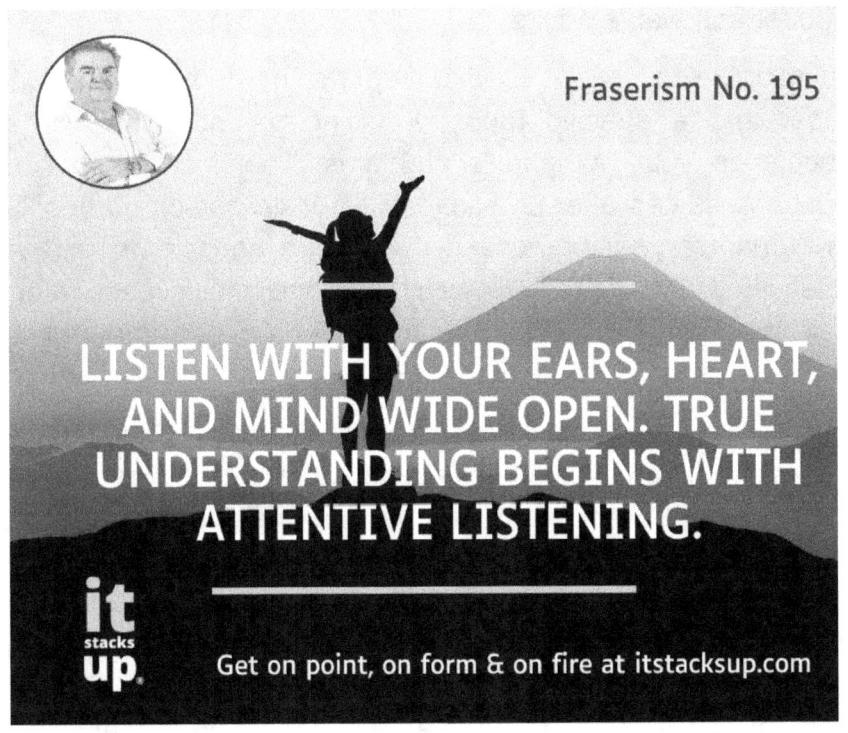

Fraserism No. 195

LISTEN WITH YOUR EARS, HEART, AND MIND WIDE OPEN. TRUE UNDERSTANDING BEGINS WITH ATTENTIVE LISTENING.

it
stacks
up.

Get on point, on form & on fire at itstacksup.com

Your FREE Item of Value

In the realm of digital marketing, offering a free item of value, also known as a lead magnet, has become a crucial strategy for improving engagement and building your email list. It's not just about attracting attention; it's about demonstrating expertise and providing something of genuine value to your audience.

Consider what you can give away or offer to encourage people to respond to your content. This could be anything from case studies and success stories that showcase your accomplishments to articles filled with hints and tips or checklists that offer actionable advice.

You might also create ebooks, reports, or booklets that delve deeper into a specific topic, providing valuable insights and solutions to your audience's problems. Tools, calculators, and spreadsheets can offer practical utility, while personal anecdotes can humanize your brand and establish a connection with your audience. Audio podcasts, webinars, and music can cater to different preferences, while presentations, slides, and demos can visually engage your audience.

Video content, including animations and 3D visuals, can captivate viewers and convey complex ideas more effectively. Software gadgets, widgets, and apps can provide interactive experiences, while live streaming event videos can offer real-time engagement. Articles that share industry knowledge or personal experiences can position you as a thought leader, while quizzes, polls, exercises, and activities can drive interaction and participation. Maps, graphics, banner ads, and images can enhance your content and make it more visually appealing.

By offering a diverse range of valuable resources and content formats, you not only attract attention but also provide genuine value to your audience, building trust and credibility while nurturing relationships that can lead to conversions and sales.

As part of your PR Campaign, you need to position yourself as an expert. You need to decide what it is you are going to be publishing and writing about that will help to demonstrate you are deeply knowledgeable and an expert within your field. You need to consider what you can give away or encourage people to respond to your "releases," articles, or stories.

You need to create a "Call to Action," "Free Item of Value" to encourage them to want to find out more about you, want to engage with you, want to buy from you or hire you. If you want good engagement and conversions, then have **Good Quality Unique Content.**

Which of the following will you use to maximise engagement and response:

- FREE Strategy call
- Ebooks on relevant topics in your industry.
- Checklists or cheat sheets for easy reference.
- **Templates** for common tasks or projects.
- **Whitepapers** offering in-depth analysis or research findings.
- **Webinars** or online workshops providing valuable insights.
- **Exclusive access** to a members-only community or forum.
- **Mini-courses** or email series delivering actionable advice.
- **Toolkits** with resources and tools to streamline processes.
- **Case studies** showcasing successful implementations or outcomes.
- **Infographics** summarising complex information visually.
- **Worksheets** to help users apply concepts to their own situations.

- **Quizzes** or assessments to gauge knowledge or skills.
- **Resource** guides compiling relevant links and resources.
- **Audio recordings** or podcasts featuring expert interviews or insights.
- **Free trials** or samples of your product or service.
- **Demos** or tutorials demonstrating product features or capabilities.
- **Access** to exclusive events or live Q&A sessions.
- **Discount codes** or special offers for future purchases.

These lead magnets and free items of value can help to demonstrate the value you offer with your products, services, and solutions, use one or integrate several of them.

Take a moment to brainstorm and decide which free item of value or lead magnet best aligns with your goals and audience needs.

Consider your industry, target audience demographics, and the benefits you can offer. Whether it's an ebook, webinar, checklist, or exclusive access to a community, choose the option that will resonate most with your audience and effectively demonstrate the value you provide.

This exercise will ensure that your lead magnet attracts the right audience and contributes to the success of your PR efforts.

Online & Offline Events

Attending, visiting, and speaking at Exhibitions, Tradeshows & Expos, along with their Virtual counterparts like online webinars, conferences, and summits, are excellent opportunities for professionals seeking to amplify their presence, network, and stay abreast of industry trends. Imagine stepping into a bustling expo hall, surrounded by booths adorned with eye-catching displays and innovative products. From the annual Consumer Electronics Show (CES), where tech giants like Google and Microsoft unveil their latest gadgets, to industry-specific conferences like the National Retail Federation's (NRF) Big Show, where retail leaders converge to discuss emerging trends, these events offer unparalleled opportunities for exposure and engagement.

Attending or speaking at these gatherings not only allows professionals to showcase their expertise but also provides fertile ground for networking and collaboration. Take, for instance, the World Economic Forum (WEF) Annual Meeting in Davos, Switzerland, where global leaders from politics, business, and academia convene to address pressing global issues. Notable figures like Bill Gates and Angela Merkel have used this platform to share insights and shape global agendas.

Moreover, online webinars and virtual summits have gained prominence, especially in the wake of the COVID-19 pandemic, offering a convenient and accessible alternative to traditional events. Platforms like Zoom and Webex have facilitated knowledge sharing and networking across geographical boundaries, enabling professionals to participate in enriching discussions and workshops from the comfort of their homes.

For aspiring thought leaders, securing speaking engagements at these events can significantly enhance their credibility and visibility within their industries. Whether delivering a keynote address or participating in panel discussions, speakers can showcase their expertise and establish themselves as authorities in their respective fields. Notable examples include Simon Sinek's TED Talk on leadership and Sheryl Sandberg's keynote at the Women in the World Summit, both of which garnered widespread acclaim and cemented their status as thought leaders.

For me, Exhibitions, Tradeshows & Expos, along with online webinars, conferences, and summits, serve as vital platforms for professionals to connect, learn, and showcase their expertise. By leveraging these opportunities, individuals can expand their networks, stay informed about industry developments, and position themselves as influential voices within their fields, gaining a competitive edge in the ever-evolving landscape of public relations.

Excellent Resources For researching Events to attend, visit & Speak at

Eventbrite (www.eventbrite.com) is a popular platform for discovering and attending a wide range of events, including exhibitions, tradeshows, conferences, and online events. Users can easily search for events based on location, date, and category, making it convenient to find relevant opportunities to attend or speak at.

Meetup (www.meetup.com) is a community-driven platform that connects people with similar interests and facilitates in-person and virtual events. Users can join groups related to their industry or profession and discover relevant meetups, workshops, and networking events happening in their area.

LinkedIn Events (www.linkedin.com/events) LinkedIn Events allow professionals to discover, RSVP to, and promote events within their network. Users can search for exhibitions, conferences, and webinars by industry, location, or date, and leverage the platform to connect with fellow attendees and speakers.

Eventful (www.eventful.com) is a comprehensive platform for discovering and promoting local events, concerts, festivals, and conferences. Users can search for events based on their interests, track upcoming events, and receive personalized recommendations based on their preferences.

Trade Show News Network (www.tsnn.com): is a valuable resource for professionals seeking information about upcoming tradeshows, exhibitions, and conferences worldwide. The platform provides detailed event listings, industry news, and insights to help users identify relevant opportunities to attend or exhibit.

10times (www.10times.com): 1is a leading online event discovery platform that offers comprehensive listings of exhibitions, trade fairs, conferences, and webinars across various industries and regions. Users can explore event details, register as attendees, and connect with organizers and fellow participants.

BizBash (www.bizbash.com): is a trusted resource for event professionals, offering insights, trends, and inspiration for planning and executing successful events. The platform features event listings, industry news, and resources to help users stay informed and connected within the events community.

Eventful Conferences (www.eventfulconferences.com) specialises in organizing industry-specific conferences and summits focused on topics like technology, marketing, and business management. Attendees can access valuable insights, network with peers, and gain practical knowledge to advance their careers.

Eventfinda (www.eventfinda.com) is a comprehensive events platform that allows users to discover, promote, and attend a wide range of events, including exhibitions, workshops, seminars, and online events. With its user-friendly interface and customizable search filters, users can easily find events tailored to their interests and preferences.

Gocadmium (www.Gocadmium.com) Gocadmium offers virtual event solutions for conferences, tradeshows, and exhibitions, providing interactive platforms for attendees, exhibitors, and speakers to engage and connect. Users can access event schedules, exhibitor lists, and educational content, making it easier to navigate and maximize their event experience.

Evensi (www.evensi.com) Evensi is an event discovery platform that aggregates events from various sources, including social media, ticketing platforms, and local listings. Users can explore a wide range of events, from local meetups to international conferences, and easily find opportunities to attend or exhibit.

The Event

he Event

Events serve as powerful tools in a PR strategy, offering unique opportunities to engage with target audiences, showcase products or services, and strengthen brand presence. However, the success of an event hinges on

162

meticulous planning and consideration of various factors. Here's a checklist to guide your event planning process:

Date of Event: Select a date that aligns with your objectives and avoids conflicts with other industry events or holidays.

Location of Venue: Choose a venue that is easily accessible, accommodates your expected audience size, and aligns with your brand image.

Price of Exhibiting: Determine the cost of exhibiting or attending and assess whether it fits within your budget.

Objectives – Leads/Sales: Define clear objectives for the event, whether it's generating leads, driving sales, or building brand awareness.

Budget for Event: Set a budget that covers all aspects of the event, including venue rental, marketing, staffing, and materials.

Other Similar Events: Research other events in your industry to identify potential competition and assess their strengths and weaknesses.

Previous Success of Event: Gather insights from past events to inform your planning process and identify areas for improvement.

Expected ROI from Event: Estimate the return on investment you expect to achieve from the event based on your objectives and budget.

Profile of Visitors: Define the demographics, interests, and needs of your target audience to tailor your event accordingly.

Profile of Exhibitors: Identify potential exhibitors or sponsors whose offerings complement your event and align with your audience.

Who Are the Speakers: Select engaging and knowledgeable

speakers who can add value to your event and attract attendees.

Why Would People Attend: Highlight the unique value proposition of your event, whether it's educational content, networking opportunities, or exclusive offers.

By carefully considering each of these factors and planning accordingly, you can ensure that your event is well-executed, impactful, and aligned with your PR objectives.

Make some notes about things you need to consider about the event:

_____

_____

_____

_____

The Venue

When it comes to planning events, selecting the right venue is crucial for ensuring success and leaving a lasting impression on attendees. Venue considerations encompass a range of factors that can impact logistics, attendee experience, and overall event effectiveness. Here's a checklist to guide your venue selection process:

Directions & Logistics: Choose a venue with clear directions and easy accessibility for attendees, whether by car, public transportation, or other means.

Access & Access Times: Confirm access times to the venue to ensure sufficient setup and breakdown time for your event.

Car Park: Assess the availability and capacity of parking facilities to accommodate attendees who may be driving to the event.

Floor Plan / Cost of Space: Review the venue's floor plan and associated costs to determine the most suitable space for your event's needs and budget.

Late Space: Inquire about the availability of additional space in case of last-minute changes or unexpected attendee turnout.

Hospitality Rooms: Consider the availability of hospitality rooms for speakers, VIP guests, or other special arrangements.

Press Area / Press Notified: Designate a press area and ensure that media outlets are notified and accommodated appropriately.

Furniture Hire: Arrange for any necessary furniture hire to enhance the comfort and functionality of the event space.

Chair Hire: Ensure an adequate supply of chairs for seating arrangements, workshops, or presentations.

Telephone Access: Verify telephone access for on-site communication and emergencies.

Toilets: Confirm the availability and cleanliness of restroom facilities to accommodate attendee needs.

Refreshment Areas: Identify designated areas for refreshments and catering services to keep attendees energized and hydrated.

Invalid Access: Ensure accessibility for individuals with disabilities, including ramps, elevators, and designated seating areas.

Cloak Room / Charges: Provide a cloakroom for attendees to store personal belongings securely, if necessary, and clarify any associated charges.

PA System: Assess the venue's audiovisual capabilities,

including PA systems, microphones, and sound equipment.

Programme / Guide: Distribute event programs or guides to attendees to provide essential information and enhance their overall experience.

Welcome Packs: Consider offering welcome packs or gift bags to attendees as a

gesture of appreciation and to enhance engagement.

By carefully considering each of these venue considerations, you can ensure that your event runs smoothly, attendees are satisfied, and your PR objectives are effectively met.

Make some notes about things you need to consider about the venue:

_____

_____

_____

_____

Stand / Booth

When planning an event, one of the key considerations is the stand or booth that will represent your brand and engage with attendees. The stand serves as your physical presence at the event and plays a crucial role in attracting visitors, showcasing your products or services, and making a lasting impression. Here's a checklist of important considerations for your stand or booth:

Shell Scheme: Determine whether you'll be provided with a shell scheme by the event organizers or if you need to arrange your own stand structure.

Tables / Chairs: Ensure you have sufficient tables and chairs for staff and visitors to comfortably interact.

Own Stand? Decide whether to invest in a custom-designed stand or utilize a standard booth provided by the event venue.

Promotional Literature: Prepare and display promotional materials such as brochures, flyers, and pamphlets to provide information about your brand.

Business Cards: Have a plentiful supply of business cards readily available for networking and exchanging contact information.

PDQ/Credit Card Facilities: Consider offering on-the-spot payment options to facilitate sales transactions.

Blue Tack / Sellotape / String: Bring basic supplies for setting up and decorating your stand, such as blue tack, sellotape, and string.

Paper n Pens: Keep pens and paper handy for taking notes, jotting down contact details, or conducting impromptu demonstrations.

Promotional Giveaways: Provide branded giveaways or

promotional items to attract visitors and leave a lasting impression.

Badge/QR Code Scanner: Utilise badge scanners to capture attendee information quickly and efficiently for follow-up after the event.

Prize Draw & Prize: Organize a prize draw to incentivize visitor engagement and collect contact information for leads.

Free Item of Value: Offer a free item of value, such as a whitepaper or e-book, to encourage visitors to engage with your brand.

Corporate Literature: Showcase corporate literature such as annual reports, case studies, or company profiles to highlight your expertise and credibility.

Carpets / Lighting / Electricity: Consider additional amenities such as carpets, lighting, and electricity to enhance the visual appeal and functionality of your stand.

Flowers / TV / Video Screen: Use decorative elements like flowers and visual displays such as TVs or video screens to attract attention and create a welcoming atmosphere.

PA System / Computing Equipment: Ensure you have the necessary audiovisual and computing equipment for presentations, demonstrations, or interactive displays.

Photographs / Stapler / Staples: Bring photographs or visuals to illustrate your products or services, along with office supplies like a stapler and staples for organizing materials.

Sweets / Mints / Name Tags: Offer refreshments like sweets or mints to visitors and provide name tags for easy identification and networking.

Till / Cash Register / Picture Hooks: If applicable, set up a till or cash register for onsite purchases, and use picture hooks for hanging displays or signage.

Leaflet Holders / Tablecloths / Jar/Bowl for Biz Cards: Use leaflet holders, tablecloths, and receptacles for business cards to keep your stand organized and presentable.

Post it Notes / Laptop / Notebook / PDA: Keep essentials like post-it notes and electronic devices such as laptops, notebooks, or PDAs for taking orders or managing inquiries.

By carefully planning and preparing your stand or booth with these considerations in mind, you can maximize your presence at events and effectively engage with your target audience.

Make some notes about things you need to consider about the venue:

_____

_____

_____

_____

Staff

When organizing an event, one of the crucial considerations is the staff involved, as they play a pivotal role in ensuring its success. Whether it's planning, managing, or executing various tasks, having a capable team can make all the difference. Here's a checklist highlighting the importance of staff and key considerations:

Planning for Event: Allocate staff members to different aspects of event planning, such as logistics, marketing, and operations, to ensure smooth coordination and execution.

Managing the Project: Designate a project manager or team lead responsible for overseeing the event's progress, addressing issues, and ensuring deadlines are met.

Stand Setup Staff: Assign staff members to handle the setup and arrangement of the event stand or booth, including assembling displays, arranging promotional materials, and ensuring everything is in place.

Promotional Staff: Employ promotional staff to engage with attendees, distribute marketing materials, answer inquiries, and promote brand awareness.

Manning of Stand: Ensure adequate staffing to staff the stand throughout the event, helping visitors, collecting leads, and generating sales opportunities.

Name Tags: Provide staff members with name tags for easy identification and professional representation of your brand.

Script for Staff: Prepare a script or guidelines for staff to follow when interacting with attendees, ensuring consistency in messaging and branding.

Appearance of Staff: Emphasise the importance of staff appearance, including attire, grooming, and demeanor, to create a positive and professional impression.

Product Knowledge of Staff: Train staff members to have comprehensive knowledge of products or services offered, enabling them to address enquiries effectively.

Following up Leads: Establish procedures for staff to capture and follow up on leads generated during the event, maximizing opportunities for conversion and relationship-building.

Rota for Staff: Develop a staffing rota or schedule to ensure adequate coverage throughout the event, accounting for breaks, shifts, and rotations as needed.

Dismantling of Stand: Assign staff members to oversee the dismantling and cleanup of the event stand or booth once the event concludes, ensuring a prompt and organized exit.

By carefully considering these staffing aspects and ensuring effective management, you can optimize the performance of your team and enhance the overall success of your event.

Make Some notes about things you need to consider about the venue:

_____

_____

_____

_____

On Stand Activities

When orchestrating an event, one of the crucial elements to consider is the on-stand activities, which can significantly impact engagement and interaction with attendees. These activities serve as magnets to attract the attention of prospects and create opportunities for meaningful interactions. Here's a checklist outlining the importance of on-stand activities and key considerations:

Live Demonstration: Conduct live demonstrations of your products or services to showcase their features, benefits, and functionality, capturing the interest of attendees.

Interactive Session: Engage attendees in interactive sessions where they can participate in hands-on activities, demonstrations, or discussions, fostering a dynamic and immersive experience.

Group Q & A: Host group question-and-answer sessions to address common inquiries, concerns, or topics of interest, facilitating dialogue and building rapport with attendees.

Mini Workshop: Offer mini workshops or educational sessions on relevant topics or industry trends, providing valuable insights and expertise to attendees.

Audio-Visual or Software Presentation: Utilize audio-visual or software presentations to deliver compelling content, visuals, or demonstrations that captivate attendees.

Free Item of Value: Provide attendees with a free item of value, such as an e-book, whitepaper, or resource toolkit, to incentivise engagement and capture leads.

Prize Draw / Competition: Organize a prize draw or competition to encourage participation and interaction, incentivizing attendees to visit your stand and learn more about your offerings.

Tablets / Mobile Devices / Laptops: Equip your stand with tablets, mobile devices, or laptops loaded with interactive content, demos, or presentations for attendees to explore and interact with.

Chairs for Mini Workshops on the Hour: Arrange seating for mini workshops or presentations held periodically throughout the event, providing attendees with a comfortable and conducive environment to learn and engage.

By incorporating these on-stand activities into your event planning strategy, you can create a dynamic and compelling presence that attracts, engages, and leaves a lasting impression on attendees, ultimately driving leads and fostering connections for future business opportunities.

Make Some notes about things you need to consider about the venue:

_____

_____

_____

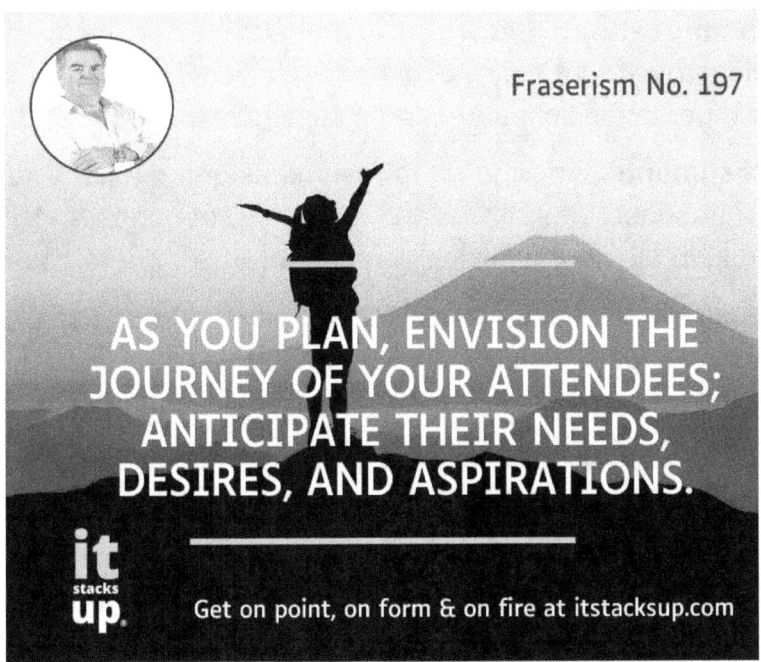

Logistics & Admin

When diving into event planning, logistics and administrative tasks often take a back seat, yet they play a pivotal role in ensuring smooth operations and a successful event. Here's a breakdown of key considerations for logistics and admin, essential for effective event planning:

Transporting of Stand: Arrange transportation for your exhibition stand to ensure it arrives at the venue safely and on time, minimizing any potential delays or complications.

Transporting of Staff: Coordinate transportation for staff members attending the event, ensuring they arrive punctually and are equipped to fulfill their roles and responsibilities.

Staff Requirements: Determine the number of staff needed for various tasks, including stand management, customer service, sales, and technical support, to ensure adequate coverage throughout the event.

Accommodation: Secure accommodation for staff members requiring overnight stays, considering factors such as proximity to the venue, amenities, and budget constraints.

Refreshments: Arrange for refreshments and meals to keep staff and attendees energized and hydrated throughout the event, catering to dietary restrictions and preferences where possible.

Subsistence: Allocate funds for subsistence expenses, such as meals, transport, and incidental costs, to ensure staff members have the resources they need during their time at the event.

Exhibition Stand: Ensure the exhibition stand is set up according to specifications and guidelines, incorporating branding, signage, and promotional materials to attract and engage attendees effectively.

Insurance: Obtain appropriate insurance coverage to protect against potential risks and liabilities associated with the event, including property damage, liability claims, and unforeseen incidents.

Order Forms: Prepare order forms or sales documentation necessary for conducting transactions at the event, streamlining the sales process, and facilitating seamless transactions with customers.

Enquiry Forms: Develop enquiry forms or lead capture mechanisms to collect valuable information from attendees, prospects, and potential customers, enabling follow-up communication and relationship-building.

Itinerary for Everyone: Create a comprehensive itinerary outlining schedules, responsibilities, and key activities for staff members and participants, ensuring everyone is informed and prepared for their respective roles and tasks.

By addressing these logistics and administrative considerations proactively, event planners can enhance efficiency, mitigate risks, and deliver a memorable and rewarding experience for all involved.

Make Some notes about things you need to consider about the venue:

_____

_____

_____

_____

Marketing & Promotion

When it comes to event planning, marketing and promotion are integral components that can make or break the success of your event. Here's why they are essential and a checklist of key considerations:

Email Existing Clients: Send targeted emails to your existing client base, informing them about the event and encouraging their attendance or participation.

Mail Existing Clients: Utilise traditional mail channels to reach out to existing clients who may not be as responsive to digital communication, ensuring maximum outreach and engagement.

Telephone Existing Clients: Personally contact key clients via phone calls to extend invitations and provide personalized assistance or information about the event.

Contact Entire Prospect List: Reach out to your entire prospect list through various channels, including email, phone calls, and direct mail, to generate interest and drive attendance.

Press Release in Trade Press: Issue a press release in relevant trade publications or industry journals to garner publicity and visibility among industry professionals and stakeholders.

Advert in Program/Guide: Place advertisements in event programs or guides to enhance visibility and attract the attention of attendees browsing through event materials.

Local Radio: Leverage local radio stations to promote your event and reach a broader audience within your target geographic area.

Chamber of Commerce: Collaborate with local chambers of commerce to leverage their networks and promotional channels for event marketing and outreach.

Press Release in Local Press: Distribute press releases to local newspapers or media outlets to secure coverage and raise awareness about your event within the community.

Local Networking Club: Engage with local networking clubs or business associations to spread the word about your event and tap into their professional networks.

Rent Attendee Mailing List: Rent attendee mailing lists from previous events or industry associations to target individuals who are likely to be interested in your event.

Promotional Literature: Create compelling promotional literature, such as brochures or flyers, to distribute at relevant locations or events and attract potential attendees.

Business Cards: Ensure all event staff have ample business cards to exchange with prospects and attendees, facilitating follow-up communication and relationship-building.

Carrier Bags: Provide branded carrier bags for attendees to carry promotional materials and merchandise, extending your brand visibility beyond the event venue.

Update Website for Event: Update your website with event details, registration information, and promotional content to drive traffic and encourage online engagement.

Lanyards: Invest in branded lanyards for event badges, offering a practical and visible branding opportunity for sponsors and organizers.

Posters: Display eye-catching posters in strategic locations to grab the attention of passersby and generate interest in your event.

Leaflets: Distribute informative leaflets or handouts in high-traffic areas to provide essential details and encourage attendance.

Signage: Use clear and prominent signage throughout the event venue to guide attendees and reinforce branding and messaging.

Postcards: Send out postcards as invitations or reminders to targeted prospects, offering a tangible and personal touchpoint for event promotion.

Promotional Clothing: Outfit event staff or volunteers in branded apparel to create a unified and professional appearance while promoting your brand.

Promotional Staff: Hire or designate promotional staff to engage with attendees, answer questions, and generate excitement about your event.

Logos: Incorporate logos prominently on all promotional materials and signage to reinforce brand recognition and association with the event.

Lunch for Clients/Prospects: Offer complimentary lunches or refreshments for clients and prospects attending the event, enhancing their experience, and fostering goodwill.

Own Branded Pens: Provide branded pens as useful giveaways for attendees, ensuring continued exposure to your brand beyond the event.

Press Packs for Press Room: Prepare press packs or media kits with relevant information and resources for journalists and media personnel covering the event.

Update Voicemail for Event: Record a customized voicemail message informing callers about your event and providing relevant contact information for inquiries or assistance.

By meticulously planning and executing marketing and promotional activities, you can maximize attendance, engagement, and overall success for your event.

Make Some notes about things you need to consider about the venue:

_____

_____

_____

_____

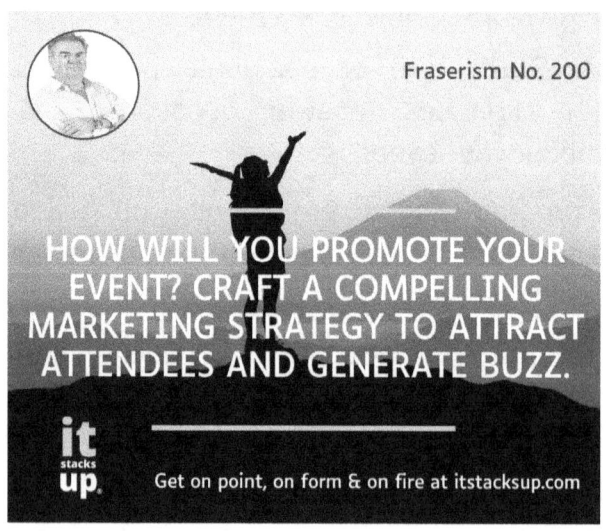

Sponsorship Opportunities

When it comes to event planning, securing sponsorship opportunities can significantly enhance your event's success while alleviating financial burdens. Here's why sponsorship opportunities are crucial and a checklist of key considerations:

Outside the Event: Offer sponsorship opportunities for branding and advertising placements outside the event venue, such as banners, posters, or signage in high-traffic areas.

Event Programme: Allow sponsors to advertise their products or services within the event program or guide, providing visibility to attendees throughout the event.

Breakout Session: Offer sponsors the chance to host or sponsor breakout sessions within the event program, providing valuable content and engagement opportunities for attendees.

Sponsor Workshops: Allow sponsors to host workshops or educational sessions related to their industry or expertise, showcasing their knowledge, and engaging with a targeted audience.

Offer to Provide Speakers: Invite sponsors to provide keynote speakers or presenters for event sessions, offering valuable insights and expertise while gaining exposure for their brand.

Event Carrier Bags: Provide sponsorship opportunities for branded event carrier bags, offering sponsors visibility as attendees carry the bags throughout the event.

Event Lanyards: Offer sponsors the chance to brand event lanyards worn by attendees, ensuring continual exposure and recognition throughout the event.

Prize for Competition: Invite sponsors to provide prizes for competitions or contests held during the event, increasing engagement and incentivizing participation.

Prize for Prize Draw: Offer sponsorship opportunities for prizes to be awarded in event prize draws or raffles, attracting attendees and generating excitement.

Event Website / Minisite: Provide sponsorship opportunities for branding and advertising placements on the event website or dedicated minisite, ensuring visibility to online audiences.

Radio Advertising: Explore sponsorship opportunities for radio advertising promoting the event, reaching a broader audience, and driving attendance through targeted marketing efforts.

By leveraging sponsorship opportunities effectively, you can not only offset event costs but also enhance attendee experiences, increase engagement, and elevate the overall success of your event.

Make Some notes about things you need to consider about the venue:

_____

_____

_____

_____

Attendee / Prospect Considerations

When it comes to event planning, understanding your attendees and prospects is essential for ensuring the success of your event. Here's why attendee/prospect considerations are crucial and a checklist of key factors to consider:

Create a Customer Avatar: Develop a detailed profile of your ideal customer, including demographics, interests, pain points, and preferences.

Update Ideal Client Criteria: Refine your ideal client criteria based on market trends, customer feedback, and changing business objectives.

FREE Item of Value to Offer: Prepare a compelling free item of value to offer attendees, such as a downloadable resource, sample product, or exclusive discount.

Prospect Database / CRM: Maintain an organised prospect database or customer relationship management (CRM) system to track interactions, preferences, and engagement levels.

Prospect Pains: Identify the pain points and challenges faced by your prospects, ensuring your event addresses their needs and offers valuable solutions.

Reasons Why Attending: Clearly articulate the reasons why attendees should participate in your event, highlighting the benefits, networking opportunities, and educational content available.

List of Product Benefits: Compile a comprehensive list of product benefits and features to showcase during the event, demonstrating the value proposition to potential customers.

List of FAQs/Objections: Anticipate common questions and objections from attendees and prepare thoughtful responses to address their concerns and build confidence in your offerings.

List of Client Testimonials: Gather client testimonials and success stories to share with prospects, providing social proof and credibility for your products or services.

Monthly/Annual Requirements: Understand the ongoing needs and requirements of your target audience, aligning your offerings with their long-term goals and objectives.

Types of Solutions Sought: Identify the specific solutions or outcomes that attendees are seeking, tailoring your event content, and messaging to meet their expectations.

Monthly/Annual Budget: Consider the budgetary constraints and spending priorities of your target audience, ensuring your offerings are accessible and appealing to their financial considerations.

Decision Maker's Name: Identify the key decision-makers within attendee organizations and personalize your outreach efforts to effectively engage with influential stakeholders.

By prioritizing attendee and prospect considerations in your event planning process, you can tailor your offerings, messaging, and marketing strategies to effectively attract, engage, and convert potential customers, maximising the success of your event.

Make Some notes about things you need to consider about the venue:

_____

_____

_____

_____

Webinars & Live Streaming Events

When organizing webinars and live streaming events, meticulous planning and preparation are key to ensuring a successful and engaging experience for your audience. Here's why considering webinars and live streaming events is crucial, along with a checklist of important considerations:

Landing Page / Video Sales Letter: Create a compelling landing page or video sales letter to attract attendees and provide essential event details, such as date, time, topic, and registration instructions.

Evergreen Video on Thank You Page: Include an evergreen video on the thank you page to further engage attendees and reinforce key event messages.

Autoresponder Nurture Sequence (3m, 2m, 1m Before): Develop an autoresponder nurture sequence to remind registrants about the upcoming event at strategic intervals leading up to the event date.

Autoresponder Nurture Sequence (4w, 2w, 1w, 1d Before): Implement another autoresponder sequence closer to the event date to increase attendance and excitement among registrants.

Social Media Posts (4w, 2w, 1w, 1d Before): Promote the event on social media platforms with regular posts leading up to the event, leveraging engaging content and visuals to capture attention.

Check Your Lighting, Sound, Microphone & Camera: Ensure optimal lighting, sound quality, microphone setup, and camera positioning on your device to deliver a professional and visually appealing live stream.

Clear Memory, Browser, Cache & Temporary Files: Prevent technical glitches by clearing memory, browser cache, and temporary files on your device before going live to maintain smooth streaming performance.

Check Backdrop / Green Screen / Virtual Background: Set up an appropriate backdrop, green screen, or virtual background to create a visually appealing and distraction-free environment for your audience.

Check Your Appearance: Present yourself professionally by grooming, dressing appropriately, and appearing polished and well-prepared for the live event.

Be On Point, On Form & On Fire: Bring energy, enthusiasm, and expertise to your presentation, engaging with your audience and delivering valuable content that resonates with their needs and interests.

By carefully considering these webinar and live streaming event considerations, you can enhance the overall attendee experience, increase engagement and participation, and maximize the impact and success of your virtual events.

Make Some notes about things you need to consider about the venue:

_____

_____

_____

_____

Running Live Streaming Events

There are several tools you can use now to reach your target audience online and run Running live streaming events has become increasingly popular in today's digital age, offering a powerful way to connect with audiences, share valuable content, and build brand awareness. Here's why considering running live streaming events is essential for event planning, along with a checklist of key considerations:

Zoom (https://zoom.us): Zoom provides a reliable platform for hosting webinars and live streaming events, offering features like screen sharing, interactive Q&A sessions, and participant engagement tools.

Be. Live (https://be.live/): Be.Live offers a user-friendly interface for creating professional-looking live streams on platforms like Facebook and YouTube, with customizable overlays, graphics, and branding options.

Google Meet (https://meet.google.com): Google Meet is a versatile tool for hosting virtual meetings and live events, with seamless integration with Google Workspace and advanced video conferencing capabilities.

Facebook Rooms: Facebook Rooms allow you to host virtual rooms for live streaming events, enabling real-time interactions with your audience and fostering community engagement.

GoToMeeting (https://www.gotomeeting.com/): GoToMeeting offers robust features for hosting webinars and online meetings, including HD video quality, screen sharing, and recording capabilities.

Dacast (https://www.dacast.com/): Dacast is a comprehensive live streaming platform that caters to businesses and organizations of all sizes, with customizable broadcasting solutions and monetization options.

WebinarJam (https://home.webinarjam.com/): WebinarJam is designed specifically for hosting webinars and live events, offering advanced webinar automation, attendee management, and analytics tools.

StreamYard (https://www.streamyard.com): StreamYard is a popular live streaming studio that simplifies the process of broadcasting to multiple platforms simultaneously, with features like multi-camera support and live chat integration.

By leveraging these live streaming tools and platforms, you can effectively engage your audience, deliver compelling content, and achieve your event objectives with ease. Whether you're hosting virtual conferences, product launches, or interactive workshops, incorporating live streaming into your event planning strategy is essential for maximizing reach and impact in today's digital landscape.

Make Some notes about things you need to consider about the venue:

_____

_____

_____

_____

Competitor Analysis

Competitor analysis is a crucial aspect of event planning, allowing you to gain valuable insights into your marketplace and identify opportunities to differentiate yourself from competitors. Here's why considering competitor analysis is essential for event planning, along with a checklist of key considerations:

Are Competitors Attending? Determine if your competitors are attending the event and assess their level of participation.

Is this Their First Time? Evaluate whether competitors are new to the event or if they have been regular participants.

Exhibition Stand: Compare and evaluate competitors' exhibition stands in terms of size, design, and visual appeal.

Promotional Literature: Analyze the quality and content of competitors' promotional materials, including brochures, flyers, and handouts.

Staff: Observe the professionalism and product knowledge of competitors' staff members.

Product Display: Assess how competitors showcase their products or services at the event.

Presentation/Pitch: Evaluate the effectiveness of competitors' presentations or pitches to attract and engage attendees.

Free Item of Value: Determine if competitors are offering any free items or incentives to attract visitors to their booths.

Volume of Stand Traffic: Measure the level of foot traffic and engagement at competitors' stands throughout the event.

Pre-event Marketing: Investigate the pre-event marketing strategies employed by competitors to generate interest and awareness.

Post-event Marketing: Investigate how competitors follow up with leads and maintain engagement after the event.

Unique Approach, Stand Out, or Memorable Moment: Identify any unique or standout tactics used by competitors to leave a lasting impression on attendees.

By conducting a thorough competitor analysis, you can gain valuable insights into industry trends, customer preferences, and competitive positioning, allowing you to refine your event strategy and maximize your impact at the event.

Make Some notes about things you need to consider about the venue:

_____

_____

_____

_____

Evaluating ROI

Evaluating the return on investment (ROI) of your event is crucial to determine its success and identify areas for improvement in future endeavors. Here's why considering event ROI is essential for event planning, along with a checklist of key considerations:

Media Coverage: Measure the extent of media coverage generated by the event across various platforms.

No. Stand Visitors: Quantify the number of visitors who stopped by your booth or stand during the event.

No. Business Cards Collected: Track the number of business cards collected as **potential leads.**

Email Addresses Collected: Record the number of email addresses gathered for future communication and marketing efforts.

No. of Qualified Prospects: Identify and quantify the number of prospects who are likely to convert into customers.

No. of Zoom Meetings/Appointments/Sales Calls Booked: Measure the success of post-event engagements, such as scheduled meetings or sales calls.

No. of Sales: Track the number of sales closed directly **because of** the event.

No. of Referrals: Assess the number of referrals received from attendees or participants.

No. of JV Partners Generated: Determine the number of potential joint venture partnerships established.

No. of New Trade Contacts: Record the number of new contacts made within the **industry.**

No. of New Media Contacts: Identify new contacts within the media industry for future **outreach.**

Perceptions of Staff: Evaluate the impressions and feedback received regarding the professionalism and knowledge of your staff.

Opinions of Stand Visitors: Gather feedback from **both** visitors regarding their experience and interaction with your brand.

Opinions of Existing Clients: Seek input from existing clients who attended the event on their satisfaction and experience.

RFIs/RFPs: Track the number of requests for information or proposals received **because of** the event.

Discount for Pre-Booking Next Event: Offer incentives for attendees to pre-book for future events.

Requesting to be Speaker/Panelist at Next Event: Express interest in speaking or participating in panels at future events.

Requesting to be Sponsor at Next Event: Explore opportunities for sponsorship at upcoming events.

Considering Hosting Your Own Event: Evaluate the feasibility and potential benefits of hosting your own event in the future.

By evaluating these metrics and considering the ROI of your event, you can make informed decisions for future event planning strategies and optimize your return on investment.

Make Some notes about things you need to consider about the venue:

_____

_____

_____

_____

Post Event

ost Event

After the excitement of hosting or attending an event, it's crucial to evaluate its impact and take appropriate actions. Here's why considering post-event considerations is vital for event planning, along with a checklist of key items:

Thank You Party/Dinner: Express gratitude to your team, partners, and clients for their participation and support.

Establish Quality of Leads: Assess the quality of leads generated during the event to prioritize follow-up actions.

Who Will Follow Up: Determine which team members will be responsible for following up with leads and contacts.

What Will be Sent/Given: Plan the content and materials to be sent or given to leads during the follow-up process.

Method of Follow-Up: Decide on the most effective method for following up with leads, whether through email, phone calls, or meetings.

Post-Event Questionnaire: Gather feedback from attendees to evaluate their satisfaction with the event and identify areas for improvement.

Identify Similar Events: Research and identify other events like the one attended or hosted for future participation or sponsorship opportunities.

Book Event for Next Year: Secure your spot for the next edition of the event if it proved to be beneficial for your business.

By carefully evaluating these post-event considerations, you can ensure that you maximize the return on investment from the event, maintain positive relationships with attendees and partners, and make informed decisions for future event planning endeavors.

 After reading the event planner above, take a moment to create your own event action plan tailored to your specific goals and objectives. Start by identifying the key tasks and deadlines associated with planning, attending, visiting, speaking at, or hosting events in your industry.

Consider the emotions you want to evoke in your audience and stakeholders, whether it's excitement, engagement, or inspiration.

By completing an event action plan, you'll not only ensure that you stay organized and focused throughout the event process but also demonstrate your commitment to delivering a successful and impactful experience for all involved parties.

Fraserism No. 201

HOW CAN YOU IMPROVE?
IDENTIFY LESSONS LEARNED
TO REFINE FUTURE EVENTS
AND STRATEGIES.

it
stacks
up

Get on point, on form & on fire at itstacksup.com

Planning Your Promotional Activities

Picture this: you've crafted a stellar PR plan complete with compelling messaging and captivating storytelling. Now, it's time to roll up your sleeves and dive into the nitty-gritty of executing those strategies. Promotional activities are the lifeblood of any PR campaign, serving as the catalyst to spread awareness, generate buzz, and drive desired outcomes.

Whether you're launching a new product, amplifying your brand presence, or positioning yourself as a thought leader in your industry, strategic promotion is key. Let's break it down. Consider the scenario of a tech startup aiming to disrupt the market with its innovative solution. To capture the attention of potential investors and customers, the startup's PR plan may include tactics like media outreach, content marketing, social media engagement, and event sponsorships.

By strategically timing these promotional activities, such as securing press coverage during product launch events or leveraging influencer partnerships to amplify brand messaging, the startup can maximize its exposure and establish credibility within the industry. Similarly, imagine a fashion brand gearing up for a major runway show during Fashion Week.

In addition to traditional PR tactics like press releases and media pitches, the brand may leverage experiential marketing initiatives such as exclusive VIP events, influencer collaborations, and behind-the-scenes content to create buzz and drive foot traffic to its showcase. By aligning promotional activities with key milestones and industry events, the brand can effectively capitalise on the heightened attention and consumer interest surrounding Fashion Week.

The importance of planning your promotional activities lies in its ability to amplify your PR efforts and achieve tangible results. By strategically selecting the right mix of tactics, timing, and channels, you can effectively communicate your message, engage your target audience, and achieve your business objectives. So, as you embark on your PR journey, remember to think strategically, stay agile, and always keep the end goal in sight.

I've listed several promotional ideas in your PR plan, now let's think about when you might want to implement PR strategies as part of your PR plan.

In crafting a PR plan that integrates both online and offline strategies, it's essential to consider the annual or seasonal opportunities that can enhance your brand visibility, engage your audience, and drive business growth. Here are some example questions and recommended online and offline PR strategies, tactics, and initiatives to incorporate into your annual or seasonal PR plan:

ANNUAL

What is the biggest trade event of the year, and will you be attending?

- Offline Strategy: Plan to exhibit or sponsor the event to showcase your brand, network with industry professionals, and generate leads.
- Online Strategy: Create pre-event buzz through social media promotions, email newsletters, and blog posts highlighting your participation.

Do you throw Christmas parties for staff, suppliers, or customers?

- Offline Strategy: Host a festive event to strengthen relationships, express gratitude, and foster a sense of community among stakeholders.
- Online Strategy: Document the event with photos and videos for social media posts and send follow-up emails expressing appreciation and extending holiday wishes.

What seasonal events or campaigns can/will you organise?

- Offline Strategy: Organize seasonal sales, product launches, or charity drives to coincide with holidays or relevant occasions.
- Online Strategy: Promote these events through targeted email marketing, social media ads, and website banners to drive traffic and conversions.

What press releases can you plan?

- Offline Strategy: Draft press releases to announce company milestones, new hires, awards, or significant achievements and distribute them to relevant media outlets.
- Online Strategy: Publish press releases on your website and share them across social media channels and industry-specific online platforms.

What promotional campaigns are you planning for Valentine's Day, Mother's Day, Father's Day, etc.?

- Offline Strategy: Create themed promotions, discounts, or offers to capitalize on seasonal spending trends and attract customers.
- Online Strategy: Launch targeted social media campaigns, email newsletters, and blog posts featuring

Valentine's Day gift guides or Mother's/Father's Day specials.

Are you organising a Summer Fun Day or Open Day?

- Offline Strategy: Host a community event or open house to engage with residents, showcase your products/services, and build brand awareness.
- Online Strategy: Promote the event through social media invites, event listings, and live streaming to reach a wider audience and encourage attendance.
- By incorporating these annual or seasonal PR strategies, tactics, and initiatives into your comprehensive PR plan, you can leverage timely opportunities to connect with your audience, generate buzz, and achieve your business objectives throughout the year.

QUARTERLY

When crafting a PR plan that encompasses both online and offline strategies, it's crucial to align your efforts with quarterly goals and opportunities. Here are some example questions and recommended quarterly PR strategies, tactics, and initiatives to guide your planning:

Q1: January - March

- What are our key objectives for the first quarter?
- Are there any industry events or trade shows happening during this period?
- How can we capitalize on New Year's resolutions or seasonal trends?

Consider:

- Offline Strategy: Attend industry conferences or trade shows to network with peers, showcase products/services, and generate leads.

- Online Strategy: Launch targeted email marketing campaigns to promote New Year's offers or resolutions, share informative blog posts related to industry trends, and engage with followers on social media platforms.

Q2: April - June

- What seasonal events or holidays can we leverage for PR campaigns?

- Are there any major product launches or announcements planned for this quarter?

- How can we integrate outdoor activities or community events into our PR strategy?

Consider:

- Offline Strategy: Host or sponsor outdoor events such as community fairs, charity runs, or sports tournaments to increase brand visibility and support local initiatives.

- Online Strategy: Launch seasonal social media campaigns with themed content, contests, or giveaways, create visually appealing infographics or videos to share on social channels, and collaborate with influencers to reach new audiences.

Q3: July - September

- What summer-themed promotions or activities can we implement?

- Are there any local or national awareness days/weeks that align with our brand values?

- How can we leverage the back-to-school season to engage with our audience?

Consider:

- Offline Strategy: Organise summer-themed promotions or contests at physical locations, host customer appreciation events or barbecues, and participate in outdoor festivals or markets.

- Online Strategy: Create engaging social media content showcasing summer activities, launch targeted Facebook or Instagram ads to promote seasonal offers, and optimize website content for mobile users.

Q4: October - December

- What holiday-themed campaigns or promotions can we develop?

- Are there any opportunities to participate in seasonal charity initiatives or sponsorships?

- How can we maximize end-of-year sales and promotions to drive business growth?

- Recommended Quarterly Online and Offline PR Strategies:

Consider:

- Offline Strategy: Decorate storefronts or offices for the holidays, participate in local holiday parades or markets, and organize customer appreciation events or holiday parties.

- Online Strategy: Launch holiday-themed email marketing campaigns with special discounts or promotions, create gift guides or holiday wish lists for your target audience, and collaborate with influencers to showcase your products/services as holiday gift ideas.

By aligning your PR efforts with quarterly goals and leveraging both online and offline strategies, you can effectively engage with your audience, drive brand awareness, and achieve business objectives throughout the year.

MONTHLY

Crafting a comprehensive PR plan that incorporates both online and offline strategies requires careful consideration of monthly opportunities to maximize brand exposure and engagement. Here are some example questions and recommended PR strategies, tactics, and initiatives to consider and include in your monthly plan:

Monthly Specific Events

- Are there any monthly-specific events or observances relevant to our brand or industry that we can leverage for PR campaigns?

Networking and Speaking Engagements

- Do we have any networking club meetings scheduled, and how can we maximize our presence or participation?
- Are there opportunities to speak at local events, workshops, webinars, or seminars to showcase our expertise and connect with our audience?

Chamber of Commerce Involvement

- Are there opportunities to engage with our local chamber of commerce, such as speaking engagements or sponsorship opportunities?

Upcoming Important Dates

- What significant dates or events are happening in the month ahead that we can tie into our PR efforts?

Content Creation (Use canva.com)

- Are we planning to write a letter to the editor or contribute guest articles to industry publications to share our insights and perspective?

Newsletter Updates

- How can we update our newsletter with relevant and timely information about our business activities, achievements, or upcoming events?

Industry Insights

- What's happening in our industry or sector this month, and how can we position ourselves as thought leaders by commenting on industry trends or news?

Media Opportunities

- What topics or issues can we offer to be interviewed about or provide expert commentary on to media outlets or journalists covering our industry?

Recommended Monthly Online and Offline PR Strategies:

Online Strategy:

- Launch targeted email campaigns to promote upcoming events or initiatives.
- Publish blog posts or articles on our website covering industry news or insights.
- Engage with our audience on social media platforms by sharing relevant content, participating in discussions, and hosting live Q&A sessions.

Offline Strategy:

- Attend local networking events or industry conferences to build relationships and expand our network.
- Participate as a speaker or panelist at relevant events to showcase our expertise and establish credibility.
- Sponsor or host workshops, seminars, or webinars to educate our target audience and demonstrate our industry knowledge.

By incorporating these monthly opportunities into your PR plan and implementing a mix of online and offline strategies, you can effectively increase brand visibility, engage with your audience, and drive business growth month by month.

WEEKLY

Crafting a comprehensive weekly PR plan requires strategic thinking and proactive engagement to maintain brand visibility and foster audience engagement consistently. Here are some example questions and recommended PR strategies, tactics, and initiatives to consider and include in your weekly plan:

Newsletter Distribution:

- Are you scheduled to send out your weekly newsletter to subscribers, featuring updates, announcements, or valuable content?

Social Media Engagement:

- Have you actively engaged with your LinkedIn or Facebook group by sharing insights, participating in discussions, or providing valuable content to members?
- Have you contributed to other relevant LinkedIn or Facebook groups to expand your reach and establish thought leadership?

Content Creation:

- Have you authored an article, blog post, or guest contribution for industry publications or online platforms to showcase your expertise and share valuable insights with your audience?

Expert Engagement:

- Have you answered questions or provided expertise on relevant expert sites, forums, or platforms to demonstrate your knowledge and build credibility in your industry?

Industry Engagement:

- Have you actively engaged with industry blogs, forums, or social networking sites to stay updated on industry trends, news, and discussions?

Sector News Roundup:

- Have you curated and shared a news roundup of relevant happenings, developments, or events within your sector or industry this week to keep your audience informed and engaged?

Recommended Weekly PR Strategies:

Online Strategy:

- Regularly schedule social media posts across platforms to maintain audience engagement and share valuable content.
- Actively participate in LinkedIn or Facebook groups by sharing insights, answering questions, and fostering discussions relevant to your industry or niche.
- Consistently publish blog posts, articles, or other content on your website to provide value to your audience and enhance your brand's online presence.

Offline Strategy:

- Attend industry networking events or webinars to connect with peers, share knowledge, and build professional relationships.
- Seek opportunities to contribute to industry publications, podcasts, or webinars as a guest speaker or panelist to showcase your expertise and reach new audiences.
- Host or participate in local community events or workshops to establish your brand as a trusted resource and engage with potential customers or clients.
- By incorporating these weekly PR strategies and initiatives into your plan, you can maintain a consistent presence, drive engagement, and strengthen your brand's reputation both online and offline.

DAILY

Crafting a comprehensive daily PR plan entails leveraging both online and offline strategies to enhance brand visibility and engagement daily. Here are some example questions and recommended PR strategies, tactics, and initiatives to include in your daily plan:

News Topic Engagement:

- What trending news topics or current events can you blog about or provide commentary on to demonstrate thought leadership and relevance in your industry?

Social Media Engagement:

- What are your friends, fans, and followers discussing or sharing on social media platforms? Can you contribute to the conversation or share relevant content to increase engagement and foster community interaction?

Follow-Up Actions:

- Have you followed up with journalists, prospects, suspects, venues, or JV partners to maintain communication and nurture relationships?

Recommended Daily PR Strategies:

Content Creation and Sharing:

- Regularly publish and share valuable content such as blog posts, articles, or social media updates that align with your brand's messaging and resonate with your target audience.
- Engage with followers and participate in discussions on social media platforms by responding to comments, sharing relevant content, and actively participating in conversations related to your industry or niche.

Relationship Building:

- Continuously nurture relationships with journalists, prospects, partners, and industry influencers by following up on previous communications, providing updates, and seeking opportunities for collaboration or partnership.
- Actively engage with relevant hashtags, topics, or discussions on social media to increase visibility, attract new followers, and establish your brand as a credible and engaged participant in your industry community.

Monitoring and Listening:

- Monitor news trends, industry developments, and social media conversations to identify relevant topics, opportunities for engagement, and potential areas for thought leadership or commentary.
- Use social media listening tools to track mentions,

conversations, and sentiment related to your brand, industry, or competitors, allowing you to respond promptly and effectively to any feedback or inquiries.

- By incorporating these daily PR strategies and initiatives into your plan, you can maintain a proactive approach to brand promotion, foster meaningful connections with your audience, and stay responsive to emerging opportunities and trends.

To finalise your PR plan, take a moment to review and analyse its components thoroughly. Identify key priorities and objectives for each timeframe, whether it's daily, weekly, monthly, quarterly, or annually. Utilise tools such as analytics platforms, social media monitoring tools, and CRM systems to track progress and measure the effectiveness of your strategies.

Look for opportunities to optimise your plan by refining tactics, reallocating resources, and adjusting strategies based on performance data and feedback from stakeholders. By continuously analysing, prioritising, strategising, and optimising your PR plan, you can ensure that your efforts are aligned with your goals and yield the best possible results for your brand or organization.

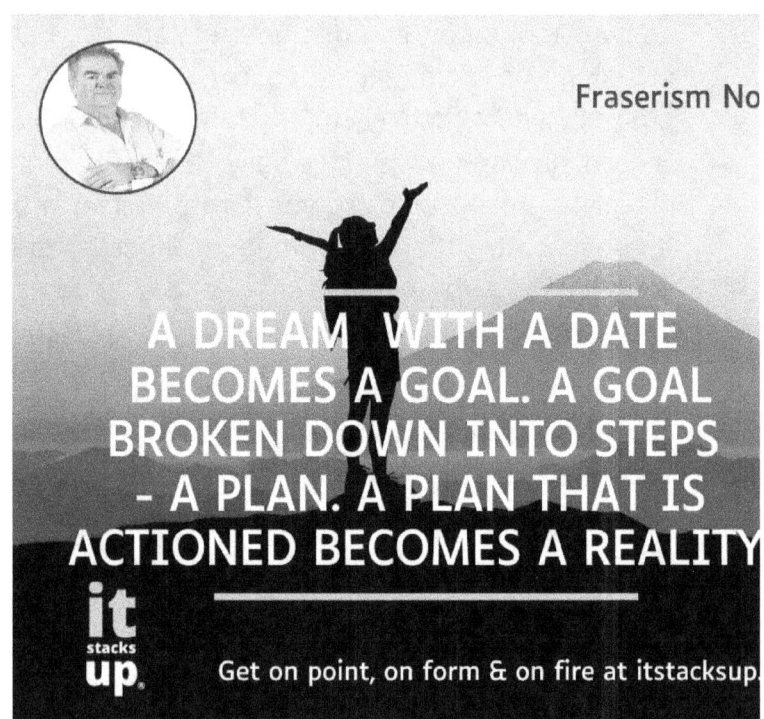

About The Author

Fraser Hay is a seasoned business coach, consultant, and keynote speaker, recognised for his multi-award-winning entrepreneurship and global impact. Having delivered inspiring keynotes on **4** continents and authored over **20+** books available on Amazon, Fraser is dedicated to empowering individuals, managers, and founders to conquer personal, professional, and commercial challenges at every stage of their entrepreneurial journey.

With an innovative approach to coaching, consultancy, and technology solutions, Fraser helps individuals and entrepreneurs realise their vision without struggle, limitation, or fear. Drawing from his experience, Fraser has identified and tackled over 2000 common issues, challenges, and obstacles encountered on the entrepreneurial journey.

Unlike traditional coaches, Fraser's methodology is grounded in practical solutions, documented insights, and guaranteed progress. Through webinars, keynotes, website, workshops, and coaching programs, he shares his wealth of knowledge and expertise to facilitate transformative growth for his clients.

As a TEDx keynote speaker with two decades of remote working experience, Fraser is committed to supporting owners, founders, and senior management teams in achieving their personal, professional & commercial objectives. He provides clarity, purpose, and measurable results, ensuring progress at every stage of the entrepreneurial journey.

Fraser's insightful quotes, (or "Fraserisms") serve as a mental espresso offering perspective and guidance to navigate life's challenges effectively.

Over the past **3** decades, Fraser has assisted entrepreneurs, managers, and business owners across the globe, spanning various industries and stages of the entrepreneurial journey. His services include strategic planning, martech, business automation and AI, accountability coaching, consultancy and keynote presentations at prestigious conferences and conventions worldwide. He also accepts a limited number of 1-2-1 personal coaching clients per annum.

NEXT STEPS? Schedule a FREE Strategy Call via his website or if you can't wait, call him on +44 (0) 1542 663491.

FREE BONUS

As promised, if you're serious about the next chapter of your life and wanting to pursue self-employment or start your own business, then you may find either of these free webinars on my website useful.

Both are available on my website at www.itstacksup.com

These webinars are practical, insightful and will help you to consider elements of your future business and marketing that you may not have thought of yet. They are fun, educational and will also challenge your thinking and existing assumptions to ensure that you get on point, on form and on fire.

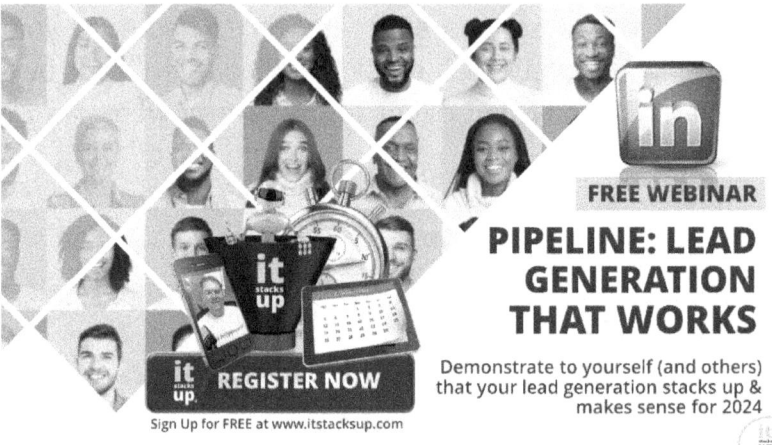

Both are available on my website at www.itstacksup.com

And if you need help, then you know where I am.

Other Work by the Author

For more, visit: www.fraserhay.com

www.ingramcontent.com/pod-product-compliance
Lightning Source LLC
Chambersburg PA
CBHW070419290526
45791CB00005B/1754